FAST WITH ME

FAST WITH ME

How to Do a 40-Day Great Lent Fast

NANETTE LANGSTON MEREDITH

RESOURCE *Publications* • Eugene, Oregon

FAST WITH ME
How to Do a 40-Day Great Lent Fast

Copyright © 2022 Nanette Langston Meredith. All rights reserved. Except for brief quotations in critical publications or reviews, no part of this book may be reproduced in any manner without prior written permission from the publisher. Write: Permissions, Wipf and Stock Publishers, 199 W. 8th Ave., Suite 3, Eugene, OR 97401.

Resource Publications
An Imprint of Wipf and Stock Publishers
199 W. 8th Ave., Suite 3
Eugene, OR 97401

www.wipfandstock.com

PAPERBACK ISBN: 978-1-6667-5737-8
HARDCOVER ISBN: 978-1-6667-5738-5
EBOOK ISBN: 978-1-6667-5739-2

11/11/22

Scripture quotations are from The ESV® Bible (The Holy Bible, English Standard Version®), copyright © 2001 by Crossway, a publishing ministry of Good News Publishers. Used by permission. All rights reserved.

I dedicate this Great Lent fast to the Lord, my Savior, who died on the cross for my sins so that I may have eternal life and peace with God.

Salvation is found in no one else, for there is no other name under heaven given to men by which we must be saved.
—ACTS 4:12

CONTENTS

Preface	ix
Introduction	xiii

About the Study		1
Chapter 1	Overall Instructions and Practical Tips for Fasting	9
Chapter 2	Spiritual Growth is the Main Aim	18
Chapter 3	Personal Daily Record Log [DRL]	25
Chapter 4	On Meditation	53
Chapter 5	On Prayer	60
Chapter 6	Juicy Tidbits to Consider	67
Chapter 7	Week 1—Into the Wilderness	72
Chapter 8	Week 2—Mind Over Matter; Spirit Over Flesh	94
Chapter 9	Week 3—Heart v. Stomach	114
Chapter 10	Week 4—The Number 40	133
Chapter 11	Week 5—Symbolic nature of Food	153
Chapter 12	Week 6—Our Body is the Temple	173
Chapter 13	Week 7—Sacrificial Love	195

Group Session Guides

Chapter 7	Week 1—Into the Wilderness	210
Chapter 8	Week 2—Mind Over Matter, Spirit Over Flesh	212
Chapter 9	Week 3—Heart v. Stomach	214
Chapter 10	Week 4—The Number Forty	216
Chapter 11	Week 5—Symbolic nature of Food	218
Chapter 12	Week 6—Our Body is the Temple	220
Chapter 13	Week 7—Sacrificial Love	222
Chapter 14	Recipe Collection and Forty-Day Sample Meal Plan	224
Bibliography		239

PREFACE

This book began with an epic, personal battle with sin. The enemy was alcohol. It threatened to consume my life if I did not stop. But for the longest time I could not, no matter how hard I tried. I was sadly addicted to drinking booze and had an extremely serious problem. I would have lost my three beautiful children, my marriage, and my very life if I had not stopped drinking booze when Jesus finally saved me from the depths of despair. I am not going to go into the dreadful details of when I hit rock bottom for the sake of the more innocent reader; I will say this, it was a life and death situation caused by my own sinful addiction to alcohol. What was a struggle against the sin of drinking too much which then turned into a desperate situation when the COVID-19 pandemic of 2020 hit. All of a sudden I was at home around the clock with all three of my boys, ages eleven, four, and two years old to homeschool. It was a living nightmare . . . and what did I turn to? More and more alcohol . . . until disaster struck; which it always does when that much booze is involved.

On top of it all, our home church was closed for the pandemic so when I needed it most, the doors were locked with nowhere to go! I felt completely abandoned, despairing and in utter defeat of life. Until Jesus showed me new ways to find and worship him, I did not know which way was up or down or right or left. I was totally lost, spiritually, even though I had been raised a Lutheran . . . went to a church just down the road nearly every Sunday growing up, baptized at age six, experienced rite of confirmation, went through communion, attended youth bible studies, all of that. I've always been part of the choir as a lead soprano singer, and been very active in the church. But something was very much missing that I didn't even know was missing until I found it. It was that personal, intimate relationship with the Lord. I thought I had it—and maybe I did to some extent—but when he rescued me from the pit of despair, forgave me my sin and shouldered the burden of it by his blood, I finally felt the grace of the free gift that he died on the cross for. No longer did I have to live in sin—constantly drinking and lying to everybody and hating myself terribly for it. No, I cried out to Jesus for help and he came down and removed that terrible, heavy sin from my very soul forever. I actually felt him take it away—the ugly, rottenness of the poison that had consumed me! Almost instantly I felt a lightness of being with that horrible weight out of my body, out of my mind—all the emotional shame and guilt I was carrying was somehow gone! An immense Joy and peace filled my inner being with an enduring promise that has never left since; one of knowing the true saving power of forgiveness that only Jesus can give us and being more grateful for it than life itself. My sobriety date is August 8, 2020, and no longer do I even think about drinking or am tempted by others drinking around me. It was a miracle! Such is his grace!

What was more, the spiritual transformation I had over the next couple years and am still having to this day, and hope I will have everyday for the rest of my life, was just starting! Like I said, our church was closed for the pandemic so I had nowhere to go and worship and pray while I got straight, so I sat outside the church in the humble outdoor chapel made of real wood logs for benches and a kind of fancy tree stump altar! It is actually incredibly beautiful because it looks directly into the Sinks Canyon into the glorious hilly mountains that reign just outside Lander, Wyoming, where I live. So, I would go there a couple days a week, for an hour each time, while I arranged a babysitter for the boys. Something in my heart, in my mind, in my soul propelled me to go there and do this, and so I did. Then, what turned into just sitting there, trying to survive, turned into prayer and meditation. It was a very natural progression and before you knew it I was praying on my knees at that little outdoor chapel and meditating with my legs crossed under me. During that whole summer of 2020 I prayed and meditated outside there while the church remained closed, getting closer and closer to Jesus and getting to know him in a way like never before. I actually became a part of the peace that surpasses all understanding. I became totally and completely filled with his Joy, serenity, awesome power and love beyond anything previously known. The Holy Spirit moved within me as I learned to trust and depend on abiding in him alone when there was nothing else. Literally, there was nowhere else to turn, nobody else to help, and nothing was open or moving except the Spirit.

But it didn't stop there. I took up the daily practice of praying and meditating at home, and I would find time away from the kids and chaos to do so. Then, in January of 2021, I was in the kitchen, just going about my day, when I heard a low, deep rumbling voice whisper, "Fast with me." I remember thinking to myself, "What? Fasting? What is fasting really, and why would I do it?" The thought had honestly never crossed my mind to undertake a serious committed fast before. Perhaps I have always had too many problems, or been too busy to consider it, but it did not occur to me until I heard the Lord's voice audibly call me to do it for Great Lent. And so I did, typical of how I do most things: headlong, all the way, dive in passionately, no brakes, etc. you get the idea. Fasting radically changed my life in so many ways and has helped enable me to stay sober as well as get rid of many other character defects I had. It has helped me be a better mother—more able to discipline our boys when they need it (which is a lot)—as well as not be so materialistic. No longer do I want to buy newer or better "things" or have an insatiable appetite for more; but am totally content in the here and now, content with what I have and just being me. Of course, it has also changed my eating habits permanently for the better and made me a healthier cook for my family. Not only did I go all in and truly learn to fast well for the Lord, following his Holy Word, but truly had a passion for it and absolutely love the ancient discipline and the fruits of the Spirit it ceaselessly brought in groves. Thus, I learned to worshipfully serve the Lord with my life, and give a spiritual offering of my body to him, through fasting, meditation, and prayer. When the church was closed for a long, long time because it was the last one to open in town—took almost a year—I learned to worship God the Father, and Jesus his Son on my own, everyday, in a very powerful way at home, or wherever I was. I even taught a yearlong class on meditation and prayer there at the church once it reopened!

I love going to church and it is extremely important, but it is also important how we live our everyday lives as Christians when we are not at church and this is what I finally was able to do. No longer did my heart desire to sin, but everything within me yearned for goodness, growth, and love. I was able to give my every waking moment, all my time, all my trust, and to honor the Lord in all that I do everyday and actually want to rather than just out of a sense of obligation. As I integrated the ancient, soulful ways of worshipping God with all my heart, mind and soul by practicing fasting, meditation and prayer everyday, there was a material change in my life. I no longer cared about things, or people, or even the world necessarily; all I cared about was my newfound relationship with Jesus, being closer to him, and having more and more peace in God. Wanting to share these lifesaving ancient ways by bringing them back to the churches is why I have worked so hard in creating this book. I want others just like me—perhaps struggling with sin or a problem that seems too hard to bear—or maybe just need to deepen their intimate relationship with the Savior, to have the tools to be able to do that on their own, or in a group Bible study. Therefore, I have written this to share my knowledge, strength, and faith with fellow believers in the body of Christ, so that they too may know the wonder and pure joy of the Lord in a whole new way. My hope is that through learning to do a Great

Lent fast, along with daily meditation and prayer, believers everywhere can and will experience the true grace and power of Jesus in their everyday, private lives. It is my goal to bring back these long lost and neglected ancient disciplines of the Bible for modern day Christians to enjoy. Anyone can experience the immense love, peace, and joy personally as it is found in Jesus offered within these practices by integrating them into our everyday living habits and routines. By faithfully fasting, meditating, and praying on a regular basis, Christians can draw near and commune with God, the Son, and the Holy Spirit on a more regular basis and not just when they are at church. All of this results in tremendous spiritual growth on so many levels, which I seek to share with people so that they too can grow in understanding of God's almighty Word, his incomparable love, and redeeming grace.

> The adverse winds blew against my life;
> My little ship with grief was tossed;
> My plans were gone—heart full of strife;
> And all my hope seemed to be lost—
> "Then He arose"—one word of peace.
> "There was a calm"—a sweet release.
> A tempest great of doubt and fear
> Possessed my mind; no light was there
> To guide, or make my vision clear.
> Dark night! 'twas more than I could bear—
> "Then He arose," I saw His face—
> "There was a calm" filled with His grace.
> My heart was sinking 'neath the wave
> Of deepening test and raging grief;
> All seemed as lost, and none could save,
> And nothing could bring me relief—
> "Then He arose"—and spoke one word,
> "There was a calm!" "It is the Lord."[1]

---

1. Cowman, *Streams in the Desert*, 186.

INTRODUCTION

This *Forty Day Lent Fast* Bible Study is made to help teach those who have never undertaken serious fasting before how to do it with confidence. It was written for any and every believer in Christ who wants to deepen their walk with him by introducing them to the ancient spiritual discipline of fasting, as it is one of the proven ways to worship and serve the Lord. Beginning with the rules of what foods can be eaten or not eaten during the forty days of the Lenten fasting season, and how to record what is eaten everyday in a handy dandy chart, to practical tips on stocking the cupboard beforehand; there is a lot of information given for every step of the way. Detailed instructions are provided for what can and cannot be eaten, and when, along with the spiritual reasons why this has been historically done throughout the Old and New Testaments. Jesus himself instituted the importance of fasting when he fasted forty days in the wilderness to overcome the temptations of Satan. Therefore, that is one of the main spiritual reasons we as Christians follow in his footsteps: to become hardened and resilient to the sins and temptations of this world so that we can remain strong, steadfast, and faithful when its wrongfulness threatens to overtake us.

Before the Great Lent Fast even starts on Ash Wednesday, there are a few things I ask readers to do in order to prepare themselves. I ask them to select three sins, or temptations, of the world out of a long list provided in *Chapter Two*, as well as five personality characteristics of self-will versus God's will from a similar list given that they would like to work on improving throughout the study. Then, I have participants circle these sins, temptations, and negative personality characteristics, as well as write them down on a piece of paper for at-home projects that we do each of the seven weeks for the sake of absolution. One of the many purposes of fasting is to help us focus on our inner, spiritual selves for a long period of time so that we can identify what sins, or temptations, or emotional blocks may be keeping us from being in closer communion with God. The ancient discipline of fasting is a powerful, biblical weapon that enables us to become humble, repentant, and able to identify our sin so that we are better able to give it over to Jesus to be taken away by the blood that he shed on the cross. But we, as believers, cannot be forgiven our sins if we do not even take the time to slow down to identify them so that we can in turn be repentant and humbly ask Jesus to remove them from us which he faithfully does each and every time. Fasting increases the power of this process so that we as followers of Christ can effectively become more completely cleansed of our sins, more purified, so that we may dwell fully in the free, gift of grace he alone gives. Restored innocence, purity, healing, joy, and rejuvenation are all gifts and benefits that may be experienced as a result.

Many other prophets and spiritual leaders from Holy Scripture employed this incredible discipline to better communicate with the Lord during hardships, purify themselves from sin, and increase the power of their prayer to be heard on high. Such examples include but are not limited to John the Baptist, King David, Moses, Ezra, the children of Israel in the wilderness, Samuel, the people of Nineveh, Esther, the apostles, and many, many more. So why don't we? Fasting has long been neglected and ill-taught by the churches, and it is my ultimate goal to bring back this old, traditional way of worshiping and serving the Lord, independently, with our bodies, our minds and our hearts. It is a wonderful, proven way to build a better, personal relationship with Christ on a daily basis, and I yearn to share all the joy, love, and purity of the Holy Spirit I myself have discovered through a few years of faithful fasting action. I know that a lot more believers today would undertake fasting if they just knew how to do it; so it is the primary goal of this *Lenten Fast Bible Study* to teach anyone and everyone who wants to embark on this wondrous journey on how to do it! A few of the tools provided are a *daily meditation and prayer guide* to help stay grounded and spiritually in touch with one self at a higher level which fasting requires. For a complete elevated experience, I include a daily scripture verse, and how it is relevant to our fasting journey each of the forty days of the fast. Also, every day I include a ten-minute meditation and prayer time, followed by questions or a topic for the *Journey Journal* that also relates to the Scripture and writing for that day.

Along with reading the daily Scripture and writing topic for each of the forty days of Lenten fasting, there is a prescribed meditation, prayer, and opportunity for writing in the Journey Journal. There are seven different themes that explore some of the main components to how and why fasting has been done by various figures and peoples throughout Holy Scripture, for each of the seven weeks of the fast. There is also a main *Virtue* cultivated specifically by fasting for each of the seven weeks. These include patience, discipline, purity, gratitude, and love for five of the weeks. And then I also discuss two of the many keys to life I have discovered through fasting, meditation, and prayer for how to lead a better, more fulfilled spiritual life in the remaining two weeks: the power of change, and temperance and moderation. Fasting teaches us how to gain moderation in other areas of our life at large by first focusing on moderation and self-control in terms of food. The lessons learned by following the rules and instructions outlined in the first couple chapters on fasting can then be applied in a variety of ways to a number of different situations and problems faced in life. For instance, moderation and self-control in financial spending and decisions, as well as help in temperance in controlling our emotions and improving how we deal with things.

A lot of attention and significance is given to the other olden ways of prayer and meditation in worshipping God with our time, bodies, hearts, and ultimately, lives. By practicing these ancient ways of the Bible—found in meditation, prayer, and fasting—everyday for an extended amount of time, we are drawing closer to God through Jesus Christ. Christians do not have to be just limited to worshipping our Abba Father on Sundays at church. This Bible study seeks to give believers a practical, do-it-yourself spiritual manual on how to practice these ancient, spiritual ways of the Bible at home, on your own. Then you can truly become more able at honoring and serving God in all that you do each day; in decisions, in action, in words, and in relationships. It is rigorous, but extremely rewarding for those who want to deepen their spiritual walk of faith with the Lord and bring him into their personal daily lives to grow exponentially upwards. I promise this as your guide along the journey: you will reap the measure that you put into it, guaranteed. It is my hope to impart to you, my knowledge, understanding, and joy of biblical fasting along this journey.

ABOUT THE STUDY

FASTING IS AN ANCIENT, biblical tool performed for a means to draw closer to God. It is a difficult spiritual discipline that was used time and again throughout the Old and New Testament, as a way to come in closer consciousness with God. Moses, Anna the prophetess, Elijah, Nehemiah, Jonah, David, John the Baptist, Ezra, Esther, Daniel and Jesus himself all fasted, just to name a few. From great prophets and leaders such as Moses and Jonah, to common worshipers as Anna the prophetess, to the Messiah in the flesh, fasting was a way of connecting to the Father. It was done for a variety of reasons but the main concept is the same today as it was in the ancient days: to go without food for a spiritual purpose devoting oneself entirely to God through this act of sacrificial worship.

This Lent Fast Bible Study is designed primarily for the individual—to be done independently on one's own spiritual journey with the Lord, Jesus Christ. The group Bible study format is included in the very back pages, and is strongly encouraged of course, but it is purely optional. The main purpose this fasting Bible study was written is to teach other Christians how to fast properly while sharing the love and joy that comes from the experience. I want to share my knowledge, gifts, wisdom, and joy on the art of fasting with fellow believers in the body of Christ. It is a neglected, lost spiritual way of the past that I strongly believe needs to be practiced more in modern times. It is my goal and purpose to impart as much as I know about the subject to you, as readers, so that you can experience it for yourself and spiritually grow, strengthen your everyday walk with the Lord, and benefit in many, many, unforeseen ways. If you can get a friend, or trusted family member to do it with you that would be awesome! Take this study around to other Christians—in your home churches or in the community—and invite them to join you in fasting for Lent, just as I have invited you to now fast with me. I strongly encourage performing this Lenten Fast with other fellow Christian believers, and trusted friends or family. But do realize it is first and foremost designed to be for the individual and kept sacred between them and the Lord. The study is set-up to be done independently—in private while devoting oneself to God. Doing it as a group bible study is purely optional, although, highly beneficial. Much fellowship would result from doing this as a group—motivation, accountability, and helpful encouragement would abound from such a setting. But it is strictly optional and not necessary to the individual's spiritual growth or overall benefit to do it in a group setting. If you want to do it in a group format you can always call in to join my home group Bible study by live Zoom streaming if you want! I will be leading the Great Lenten Fast here in my community, and you are all, of course, invited to join via Zoom. However, it is more powerful to be in person and have someone you can swap information with, if possible. Information for how to join my Great Lent Fast bible study via Zoom with the right password and User ID can be found on my blog at: *https://greatlentandnativityfasting-org.ghost.io*.

For the purpose of this study we will focus on the fact that Jesus fasted in the wilderness for forty days. The Great Lent fast is also forty days long and echoes that desolate time of suffering Jesus spent in the wilderness before he came out and was tempted by the devil. "Then Jesus was led by the Spirit into the wilderness to be tempted by the devil. And after fasting forty days and forty nights, he was hungry. And the tempter came and said to him, "If you are the Son of God, command these stones to become loaves of bread" (Matt 4:1). So, one of the main reasons Jesus was led by the Spirit into the wilderness and fasted for forty days was to be able to overcome temptation and not give in to sin. Thus, this is one of the main purposes we will dwell on in this Great Lent study; that of recognizing worldly temptations, overcoming them by building up our spiritual weapons, and when we do sin, acknowledging our sin and giving it fully over to the Lord so that he can forgive us. The devil tempted Jesus but he did not give in to the temptation and sin because he was strong and perfect after fasting forty days. But we are weak and cannot resist temptation and give in to it and do actually sin. "If we say we have no sin, we deceive ourselves, and the truth is not in us. If we confess our sins, he is faithful and just to forgive us our sins and to cleanse us from all unrighteousness. If we say we have not sinned, we make him a liar and his word is not in us" (1 John 1:8–10).[1] So fully acknowledging what sins are first of all, and then giving them up to the Lord is a big part of the fasting process during this season of repentance. We desire to cleanse ourselves of our sin by confessing and repenting of them to Jesus, who died on the cross, so that he may forgive our sins and bring us into further grace and peace with God.

Just as Jesus fasted in the wilderness to overcome sin and temptation, so can we follow his example to become more like him in resiliency and

---

1. Unless otherwise indicated, Scripture quotations are from the ESV Bible.

strength against sin by fasting for lent. So, let us follow him into the wilderness of fasting for forty days in an incredible personal journey of endless promise! What does it mean to follow Christ? We are his sheep and he is the Shepherd. "When he has brought out all his own, he goes before them, and the sheep follow him, for they know his voice" (John 10:4). It means to deny yourself and take up your cross even to the point of death. Well, fasting is a way of denying oneself and selflessly relying on Christ for our daily needs. True, one does not die (or even come close to it, don't worry) by fasting, but it is a way of suffering alongside Jesus on the cross. It demonstrates a willingness to take up the cross in remembrance of what he did for each of us and to give up something important to us—namely food and our sin.

This "giving up" aspect of Lent can also be interpreted as sacrifice. Jesus demonstrates his love for the Father and for us by sacrificing his own life. It is the greatest kind of love that exists—the laying down of one's own life for that of someone else. This divine love exists between the Father and the Son, just as it exists between Jesus and us. He says, "I am the good shepherd. I know my own and my own know me, just as the Father knows me and I know the Father; and I lay down my life for the sheep . . . For this reason the Father loves me, because I lay down my life that I may take it up again. No one takes it from me, but I lay it down of my own accord. I have authority to lay it down, and I have authority to take it up again" (John 10: 14–18). God knows Jesus like a parent knows their child and Jesus knows us in the same way. We belong to him; we are his sheep. He didn't have to give up his life on the cross so that we could be forgiven our earthly sins and have peace with God. He did it out of sacrificial love for us—he *wanted* to—and that is one of the many reasons God loves him so much. Because he was obedient to the point of death to what the Father sent him to do—die for the sins of humanity and restore peace, grace, and mercy between the Creator and the creation. So what can we sacrifice or "give up" for Lent out of love for the Lord? Giving up food and other sins, or interferences, or past problems, is a great way to show our love for Christ and what he did for us.

Another main purpose to fasting during the Season of Lent can be to recognize that we are God's temple and we are to worship and honor him at all times, in all ways. "Do you not know that you are God's temple and that God's Spirit dwells in you? If anyone destroys God's temple, God will destroy him. For God's temple is holy, and you are that temple" (1 Corinthians 3:16–17). Thus, we are not just to worship him in the visible temple of church but in our everyday, private lives. We are the temples as we journey throughout our worldly homes, carrying the church with us. Fasting is an incredibly powerful spiritual tool that we can employ in our private, spiritual lives. It is a way of worshiping and honoring God similar to prayer and meditation. God sees everything we do in private and in our everyday life. People see what we want them to see; namely at church and in other public places. So we as Christians need to line up the way we are living everyday with the Word of God and what is preached on Sunday. But we do not have to be at church to be in communion with the Lord. We can be closer to him anywhere—at our homes, at work, at the park with the kids, all day long, every day! Fasting is something we as Christians can do to enhance our spiritual lives and grow everyday closer to the Lord! It helps align us with the truth when everyday life gets in the way. True, the world around does not know what we are doing, but he who sees everything we do does and will reward us. Prayer and meditation are the same way, and I strongly recommend doing both alongside fasting during the study. You do not have to just confine them to church! But by practicing these powerful spiritual tools on a daily basis—fasting, prayer, and meditation—we grow in faith, humility, integrity, and honesty. We become a lot closer to the Savior and have more peace and grace with God. We can employ these spiritual tools anytime anywhere to overcome the temptation to sin, and come into instant contact with the Spirit inside us. Much can be accomplished through this walk of faith, trusting in the Spirit of the good Shepherd who always leads. We can serve him greatly in our everyday lives by sacrificing our time, our bodies and our energy to fasting, prayer and meditation. Worshiping him anytime, anywhere gives the body a sense of comfort and security in the eternal life; knowing that we can be at One with him whenever or wherever we are and not just at church or with a priest. Our body is the temple of God and his Spirit goes with us wherever we go so let us give ourselves over to humble, more subtle acts of servitude that are nonetheless very brave in our daily life. All it means is more Jesus, which means more God, which means more grace and abundance in all ways!

Why are there always forty-six days between Ash Wednesday—the start of Great Lent, of course—and Easter Sunday; yet only forty days of fasting for this holy period? Well, let me tell you! You are lucky you are reading this before fasting for Lent because when I first did it I had not yet figured out this mystery and ended up fasting for the full forty-six days and wondered why! So, after much research and deliberation I have found that Sundays are considered to be free days to Christians who fast during this time around the world, and so are excluded from the forty-six day total count. Thus, we will be fasting Monday through Saturday throughout the entirety of Lent, but not on Sundays. Sundays are free from fasting according to how Christians have long celebrated them as free, feast days in preparation for the Resurrection Day of Christ; the greatest feast day of all!

It is my promise, from the heart, that if the fasting rules are strictly kept, as much as possible, then great rewards will come to you. Fasting biblically has the power to change lives! Get rid of old habits and character defects completely from the person and replace them with altogether newer, better habits and traits! Your life can be spiritually transformed if the rules and instructions are properly followed, and I guarantee a positive enhancement to everyday Christian living as a result. As long as you surrender as much as possible to embrace the process, many wondrous virtues will be further cultivated along the way. Faith, hope, love, purity, discipline, self-control, honesty, joy, happiness, and better health are some of the many immense spiritual gifts that this ancient spiritual discipline grows in the soulful heart. A much closer, personal relationship with the Lord, Jesus Christ, also develops as a result of fasting properly for forty days. Greater self-worth in being a Christian and living out our everyday faith, principals, and blessings is found and truly felt anew. Much renewal and growth in the faith becomes known as fasting is integrated into everyday life choices. Great wisdom comes in the revelation of God's Word as well, as believers gain a new perspective on Scripture as they themselves experience what many other infamous prophets and followers of Christ—as well as the Lord himself—did in fasting. The Word absolutely becomes alive and living all the more powerfully when we fast, since this spiritual discipline opens our eyes to deeper meanings and hidden truths. We read about prophets and others who have fasted with a newfound appreciation as it brings us so much closer to the power of God in Spirit, Word, and the all-consuming joy of truth. I personally promise all the effort you put into this incredible journey will be returned to you ten fold.

THE RULES

#1. Absolutely No Alcohol
#2. No Social Media posting —(unless it's to a site with people specifically devoted to fasting for Christ)
#3. Write down any and everything you eat in the Daily Record Log *and at what time* you ate it

Reasoning Behind the 3 Cardinal Rules:

The first and most important rule is absolutely no alcohol during strict Christian fasting rule. I do this because I think it is dangerous for the body, mind, and spirit to ingest any alcohol while fasting because it will affect someone even more greatly and detrimentally. When one drinks wine on an empty stomach it is much more severe on the system, and therefore could result in more dire, unwanted consequences. Plus, people tend to not moderate their alcohol intake at times and the consequences could be fatal and lead to terrible disasters if these mishaps or bad habits were done without food in the stomach. Therefore, absolutely no alcohol should be drunk, besides wine taken at communion, during this strict, biblical fast. Alcohol and fasting are a dangerous, potentially lethal combination. Please, please beware and heed this warning. If you are going to follow one rule above all others, and stick to it, make it this one. I make it to protect you because even though we have perhaps never met I love you. By far, this is the most important rule in this serious undertaking!

The reason for no social media of any kind (except to sites exclusively dedicated to *Christian* fasting) in this regard, specifically during the time of Lent, is because it clearly warns against this very thing in the Bible. Scripture is adamant that fasting is to be done in private, with only God the Father knowing. Now, if we are doing this as a Bible study together—as a collective Body of Christ—then of course we will know who the participants are, but that is still for the glory of God. It is being known and shared in a protected, safe environment still ultimately overseen by the Lord. But we are not to make a big deal of it to others and go around "showing off" our secular ways. This is one of the only actual instructions Jesus himself gives to his followers in regards to fasting so we must take it extremely seriously. Everything he said was for a reason and to protect us, and this is a very clear rule he gives in regards to this ancient discipline. For it states: "And when you fast, do not look gloomy like the hypocrites, for they disfigure their faces that their fasting may be seen by others. "Truly, I say to you, they have received their reward. But when you fast, anoint your head and wash your face, that your fasting may not be seen by others but by your Father who is in secret. And your Father who sees in secret will reward you" (Matt 6: 16). Those are the instructions for how to fast from Jesus himself. It is extremely important to follow this basic, cardinal rule. Basically, we are to disguise this very important, central, spiritual element of our very selves from the outside world. Rather, look your best and put on a smiley happy face so that nobody would know that you may be painfully hungry inside at times; so as they might ask you; "What is wrong?" Instead, discover the real spiritual you and be that way, regardless of how your flesh feels. Be filled with love, happiness, vitality, faith, and joy so someone might ask; "How are you that way?" And certainly do not broadcast it across the Internet! That is why there is no social media posting because that is broadcasting it to the outside world, to be seen by others and not in private for the glory of God.

However, there are exceptions to this rule . . . it is fine to *tell* others that you are fasting when you feel prompted by the Spirit to do so. Yes, by all means, share your faith, but that is done by word of mouth, and not by blogs or Facebook or just putting it out for anyone to see on social media. It is encouraged to share with those chosen few people in your life whom you love and trust when feel prompted by the Spirit to do so. Just please, for your own protection, do not go posting what you are undertaking and doing to the whole technological world indiscriminately. Another exception to this cardinal rule is to post to sites exclusively dedicated to Christian fasting with people who are actively involved in this practice. As the leader of this ministry I have to do this constantly—*on my blog or sites dedicated to this practice* —in order to spread the Word of God and reach people it might help. The difference is the motivation and intention in our hearts while we post that makes this exception okay. While we are posting to a site dedicated to Christian fasting, such as mine, we are simply sharing our faith in goodness and truth with others, which results in fellowship. Likewise, when we are joined together by group bible studies, we are supporting one another in faith, in fellowship. All this is to the glory of God. I make this rule to protect you and reinforce the instruction Jesus gave to us all. Do not open yourself to be questioned mercilessly or possibly ridiculed by those who most likely do not understand the first thing about fasting in the Bible. It would be asking for trouble.

The third rule magnifies the power of the written Word in practice. There is something very important that goes on in the mind processes from actually recording what you eat and drink each day. The recording of these essential facts of life is extremely conducive to having a successful fast. It also builds honesty, accountability, and moral integrity. The Personal Daily Record Log (DRL) becomes one of the main constituents for the basis of our shared experience. It gives us a place to start, to compare, to discuss, to laugh over, to come together in harmony over hot vegetable broth. The DRL is the only thing that we may, if we so choose, physically pass over to somebody else and share in small groups. We do this for two main reasons: to motivate each other to fast as well as build unparalleled honesty.

It is motivating to trade DRL's and compare notes with fellow fasters but, again, this is merely optional and not a necessity. However if you can find someone to check in with, be accountable to, and engage in this shared experience it can be valuable and very rewarding fellowship. Try to share this message in your church—and offer the opportunity for others to join in for further interest! There is much to discuss in fellowship as to what temptations from the pantry are nearly impossible to resist, or what the top preferences are for non-dairy over milk . . . Not to mention how hard it can be going without food for long periods of time and what one does to avert the temptation to eat . . . How one needs the warmth of fellowship and people to gather round the fasting fire! The DRL serves as an ultimate testimony dedicated in truth to God and should be appreciated as such. It is a written record that can be pulled out at any time to share with a friend or reference for the future. They are also really good to self analyze for improvement over progressive fasts. The DRL is a phenomenal tool in your spiritual weaponry kit to combat evil. Most importantly the DRL cultivates honesty and integrity in the individual's personal walk with the Lord. Do not lie or make stuff up because it is pointless. He already sees and knows everything that passes your lips! The paramount purpose of the DRL is that it is dedicated to the Lord—designed to be a witness testimony between you and he—one of truth. It is useless to try and hide things from the Lord, so be honest and allow yourself all the best opportunities to grow in faith and integrity upwards in Christ.

Now, if you do break the strict fasting rule and eat when you're not supposed to (or any another one of the three cardinal rules) it is not like in Gremlins when he broke the rule of feeding Gizmo after midnight and you will boil over and spawn into slimy, man-eating monsters . . . just make a note of it in your *Journey Journal* or DRL and use it as a lesson to learn by, and as an opportunity to grow in honesty and faith.

As far as some of the spiritual aims that I provide in the study is the main theme of humble repentance from sins and *giving up* your sins, temptations, and/or bad habits along with *giving up* food. Now, if this does not appeal to you or perhaps you have an even bigger problem situation that you are trying to deal with in your life right now (such as a medical diagnosis, a problem with a child or spouse, the loss of a loved one, or whatever the individual case may be), feel free to make this your personal main theme for Lent fasting. Then, whenever you come across a place in the study where I ask you to list, or deal with your sins/temptations, simply replace that with the issue you are *giving up* to the Lord with holiness. This truly could be anything that you feel an incumbent need to receive help with from God. It could just be something personal in your life, that you know needs to change, but you have not the strength or willpower to change it alone and need our Father's help. Write that great something that needs changed down when you come to chapter 2 in lieu of the sins and temptations if you would rather fast to the Lord for this instead. Then remember to recall this personal issue and substitute it for the sins/temptations whenever I ask participants to list or do something with these throughout the study.

CHAPTER 1

OVERALL INSTRUCTIONS AND PRACTICAL TIPS FOR FASTING

All Weekdays and Saturdays of Lent: No animal products: no meat, no eggs, no fish, no dairy (few exceptions allowed), no alcohol, no highly processed foods, no more than 6 teaspoons or 24 grams sugar per day for women and no more than 9 teaspoons or 36 grams sugar daily for men.

Only one, humble meal is allowed in the evening for each of the forty fasting days of Great Lent. The meal should be enjoyed in a single sitting and not spread out for more than an hour. Absolutely no snacking or other eating out of this hour-long time frame allowed each evening. There is one, 20oz. vegetable drink allowed each fasting day. This needs to be store bought and not a smoothie made at home. I recommend V8, Odwalla *green machine*, or any other green, vegetable-based 'smoothie type drink.' This is the strict Christian fasting rule. Sundays are free days so the fasting rule does not apply, although, please read carefully the precautions and helpful tips given on the first two Sundays.

Note on Dairy: Although there is technically no dairy allowed, a few *extremely* minimal allowances are okay; not to exceed by more than 2 Tablespoons per day: (i.e. a spoonful sour cream atop soup, a sprinkle of cheese on a salad, a spoonful of creamer in coffee, although there are a wonderful array of non-dairy creamers that are delicious). Also, I consider *bread* to be negligible when it comes to dairy, so bread is allowed.

The rules were derived from the strict Fasting Rule of the Orthodox Church that I used as a basic guideline when I first started fasting. Over the years I have adapted and modified it slightly to make it more suitable for contemporary life. For instance, the strict Orthodox Fasting rule says no butter or oil, but I allow it because I personally don't see any reason for excluding it. Keep in mind, I have altered, added, and modified these rules over the years, so adhere to the ones written in this study, recorded above. Another example of how these rules are different is that I added the allowance of one 20oz. vegetable drink per strict fasting day because I think it is important to stay healthy and well nourished and one can never have too many vegetables!

"The Church has always exempted small children, the sick, the very old, and pregnant and nursing mothers from strict fasting."[1] For the purpose of this Great Lenten Fast the same exceptions apply. Basically, you must be fairly healthy and in the sixteen to seventy-five-years-old age bracket; and neither pregnant or nursing. I would say an exception for health problems, but fasting can actually help cure many health problems, so if you have an underlying condition please consult your doctor before undertaking this fast, but do not entirely rule it out yet. Another exception is for those that have ever struggled with an eating disorder, or have sought medical help for Anorexia Nervosa or Bulimia Nervosa. If you are going to attend my Lenten Fast Group Bible Study via Zoom I will be allowing a time to ask specific questions regarding certain health issues that may or may not allow one to partake in the fast from that day forth. However, I will not be held responsible for people going astray in fasting who do not follow the rules, are doing it for the wrong reasons, or fail to observe the *exceptions*.

PRACTICAL TIPS FOR FASTING

You are probably wondering. . . well, what can I eat then? Sit back, get comfortable, and make yourself a hot drink and get ready to be amazed because it is incredible how many doors of variety of nutritious splendor in abundance will be possible for you within the strict fasting rule! Fear not dear believer because I promise not only will other more delicious dishes become open to your palette, but you will break old habits of unhealthier eating and replace them with better, newer ones. New foods and alternative substitutes shall present themselves to your discerning eye in a parade of colorful tastes. Do not be afraid for it is still a land of plenty, although just slightly more selective and higher in quality. The benefits are immeasurable and can last a lifetime, resulting in better health, nutrition, and overall greater knowledge in the possibility of food.

---

1. The Fasting Rule of the Orthodox Church, "Exceptions," line 1.

For the most part, drinks are unlimited, however, with a big catch. In order to stay within the strict fasting rule regarding sugar, you cannot exceed the allotted daily amount, so that right there will automatically significantly limit your drink intakes and what you can drink. You will be shocked at how much sugar is in drinks (and any dessert-type food). For instance, there are 58g of sugar in a 16oz. vanilla soy latte, so this is not even an option! That is more than twice the amount of sugar allowed for a woman faster, and even way above the amount prescribed for men. However, do not be afraid, O children of God, for you can still get a 16oz. soy latte, which only has 8 grams of sugar, sans the flavor and maybe add your own little sweetener to it or ask for sugar-free flavors! It will still taste perfectly lovely and you will feel better enjoying it than if you were consuming way too much sugar . . . These type of daily differences in how you do things will help you become creative and learn to do the same things you usually do but just in a slightly different way. Fasting will teach you to explore avenues untraveled before in the grocery store or restaurant. It will show you to branch out and simply try new things instead of staying in the old comfort zone. It forces one to deliberately and faithfully change eating habits to fit within these strict fasting guidelines, but I promise it is not only doable but incredibly worth it. You will be amazed at how well the body does with one meal a day on super delicious, rich, healthy food! You do not know until you try!

I recommend stocking up on non-dairy milk such as soymilk, coconut milk, almond milk, oat milk or rice milk. Get a non-dairy creamer for coffee. Espresso drinks, hot chocolate, chai, well pretty much any hot drink like that is still allowed while fasting but must be made with non-dairy milk (and keep diligent track of the amount of sugar and do not exceed it!) Keeping track of sugar is paramount and an important part of the strict fasting rule. You will need to look up how much sugar is in everything you would normally drink, and perhaps eat, although drinks are the biggest culprit, and recalibrate your choices. Hot tea, hot broth—vegetable, not chicken or beef (no animal products) —are great choices! I really like a cup of hot apple cider. Just be sure to record *everything* you eat or drink in the DRL, with the *exact* time eaten for food. For drinks, you do need to record everything drunk, but not the times. Enjoy that one 20oz. green, or red, vegetable smoothie/juice drink each day. I recommend Spicy Hot V8 and the cheaper version of Odwalla's *Green Machine*—the Bathouse's *Green Blend*. These vegetable smoothie/juices should be easy to spot at any main grocery store with the other smaller bottled smoothies usually found by the produce section. The reason I want you to buy this at the store is to prevent you from temptation from making them during the day at home. Plus, it is easier to measure and not waste any unnecessary ingredients if you just buy a big container of V8 or other vegetable juice blend and simply pour it out when you need it at any time during the day. This 20oz. of daily allowed vegetable drink helps the body sustain the necessary energy until the one, humble meal in the evening. In the meantime the faster cultivates the immense virtues of self-discipline, patience, honesty, integrity, self-control, selflessness, humility, and faith.

Now, for the much more extensive subject of food . . . personally, my go to meals are beans with whole grain chips on top or a nice, hot bowl of soup accompanied by fresh baked baguette bread. The choices in soups are endless and my favorites are the brand '*Amy's*' in the varieties of split pea soup, golden lentil, black bean soup, vegetable barley, no chicken noodle soup (yes, that is actually what it's called), and vegetarian chili—which I never knew existed either before fasting! Any type of fresh baked bread is always a must and goes beautifully with all kinds of soups. Whole grain rice, pasta, tortillas, bread, and chips are a must as well. Cook up some whole grain rice and add some beans, enchilada sauce, salsa, and a *spoonful* of sour cream on top. Go heavy on vegetables and fruit when you do eat because these are obviously the best foods for you and also replenish necessary nutrients and energy. Believe me, you will be so hungry by the time evening rolls around that a big plate full of vegetables and fruit will look like a Godsend from heaven! Refer to the sections on *Recipes*, *Sample 40-day Meal Plan* in the back of this book, and the example of my personal DRL for continual help on what to eat and for help planning meals.

That is one of the greatest secrets of fasting in regards to how it intrinsically promotes nutrition and better eating: the faster becomes so hungry as the day wears on without anything to eat, that when evening finally does roll around truly *anything* is welcome, satisfying, and all too delicious. It doesn't matter what it is when you are hungry enough . . . you will be so grateful and overjoyed with all the weird health nut squirrel food you've perhaps snubbed forever as belonging to a different species of human until now! That's right . . . introduce quinoa, granola for dinner, mighty salads, vegetarian sandwiches, delicious hot vegetable dishes, bread galore, chickpeas, couscous, nuts, rich avocadoes, the list goes on and on. Now, we as fasters just get to be creative and put together new combinations of things we have perhaps been avoiding eating for far too long. Perhaps we have condemned many "health nut" foods without actually ever trying them. Now is the time, today is the day, seize the opportunity to try new things! I know change is hard, but it is a necessary component of life. Believe me, these simple, modest foods may seem too basic and not what you would want . . . but . . . you will! The longer you go without food during the day the better cucumbers, bread, and all whole, simple, foods appear. Vegetables and fruits never looked so glamorous and divinely tempting as when you have not had a bite to eat for nearly twenty-four hours. It works like magic! It is way easier than you might think. Trust me, you will be fine. Think of favorite foods within the limitations and stick to those for the duration of the fast! After all, a diet is defined as a pattern of eating so once you have found a few staples that you like and are satisfied with, just repeat those and add a new one, and repeat, etc. I remind you, this is not a diet; but I am trying to help you to fast by understanding concepts in eating so that you may do so successfully.

Don't forget about banana chips, nuts, crackers, croutons, seeds, and other supplemental delicacies to add to soup, salad, or any meal to enhance the appetite. I really like to add croutons to soup as well as salad, along with a piece of bread. And that should be enough! Keep it simple! There is way too much hype and complicating food and diets these days. The key is simplicity. Food is a whole, simple entity made by God. Just take it for what it is and don't over think too much about it. Food is beside the point, anyways, as you will learn to understand later on in the study. So, be modest, be simple, and humble about that one meal taken at night for that is the spirit of things. No posting elaborate alternatives or fancy recipes. Enjoy it with a newfound gratitude and allow yourself to grow in accordance with God's Holy Word.

LEVELS I-IV OF FASTING FOR CHRIST

Through my experience of doing forty-day fasts, and other fasts of varying duration through the years, I have come up with a system that will hopefully help motivate others while fasting. Please, always keep in mind that these are *not meant* to encourage any kind of competition amongst fasters. Any spirit of competition or comparison between believers while fasting for Christ is absolutely contrary to the Holy Spirit. The Levels are also designed as a pedagogical tool for helping me coach individuals at a given level and helping them gain confidence to sustain that one, while eventually approach the next with time and experience. In other words, it helps track a person's journey and be able to know where they're at along the way for communication purposes. The four different levels of strict Christian fasting are as follows:

Level I

Eat one meal per day, in the evening, for the duration of the fast, following the given *rules and instructions* explained in the previous sections.

Level II

Skip a meal and go for 48-hours without food. Then go back to the one meal every night for as long as you like. Repeat again, and either do the same forty-eight-hour length of time absolute fasting, or try to go for longer and longer periods of time without eating. For instance, once you skip a nightly meal and make it into the second day, you can either eat one meal (taken all during the same sitting) that evening for a forty-eight-hour fast, or wait until later and later in the evening, increasing the time you go without food. Waiting later in the evening to have that one meal could result in any number length fasting periods: forty-nine-hours, fifty-hours, fifty-six-hours, etc. until it reaches midnight or its bedtime. Once the clock turns to the next day there is no eating allowed until evening of the next day. That is the rule for strict fasting.

The caveat to this decision is that you must wait until evening to eat anything to stay within strict Christian fasting guidelines. If you do not eat anything that second night, then you've got to strive for the seventy-two-hour long fast and go all day without eating. The concept to remember in fasting at Level II is that when you decide to skip a meal and go for a longer period of time without eating, you've got to strive to go just a little longer than you did the last time! This creates endurance in the body, and builds up resilience and strength in the overall process. Then when you do eat again, you can go back to the one nightly meal for as long as you like or feel a return of comfort. Then, when the faster is ready to challenge themselves for a little longer absolute fasting period than they did previously, they hold fast to Christ and just do it in a leap of faith!

Level III

There are no two meals in a row on this Level of strict Christian fasting. Then, when food is taken again in the evening after the minimum of a forty-eight-hour long fast, try to go as long as you can without eating anything. This can either be another 48-hours because remember, there are no 2 meals in a row here, or the faster can go far as long as they can prevail, for days if they can. Then, when you absolutely must eat, have the one meal in the evening and go again for as long as you can without food—with the minimum of time between meals being forty-eight-hours. This pattern just repeats itself for the entire forty-days of Great Lent or Nativity season: eating a meal at night, and then going forty-eight-hours (or as long as you can); eating a meal at night, and then going a minimum of forty-eight-hours again; eating one meal, and so on and so forth.

Another important last point to fasting at Level III is that you don't necessarily have go to further than your last period of time without food, which is a defining feature of Level II fasting. For instance, if you just fasted for seventy-two-hours, and had the one dinner meal, you can go back to forty-eight-hours between meals which means simply skipping the next night's meal, and eating the day after. Verily, I promise you it is not as hard as it sounds! When you get in the groove of it, your body will naturally adjust accordingly and find it easier and easier. The purpose of fasting at this extreme level is to push the body past normal limits and dwell entirely in the Spirit. To be more like Christ in how he went forty-days without any food in order to overcome the temptation of sin is the ultimate goal. So, with bigger and bigger steps, we as fasting Christians, challenge ourselves to be more like him in our decisions, actions, and love.

Level IV

Jesus and Moses!!! Maybe Mahatma Gandhi? Jesus when he fasted in the wilderness forty-days without eating *anything* before being tempted by the devil. Moses fasted forty-days without eating *anything* before receiving the Ten Commandments on Mt. Sinai.

So, now, after having reviewed the four Levels of fasting, please take the time to consider at what Level you will be doing this forty-day fast. If this is your first time fasting —which for most of you it will be—then you need to do Level I for the entire duration of the fast. Even if you have perhaps done a fast before, if you have not done a forty-day long one, then please consider containing yourself to Level I to start with, until you get some experience under your belt before attempting the higher Levels. With more experience and time spent fasting, the further you will be able to advance in Levels. Fasting is very similar to any sport, or any skill . . . practice makes perfect! The more you do it, the longer you do it, and the integrity you do it with makes you better and better at it—allowing your body the spiritual training to go for longer and longer time without food. But unlike any sport, it does not matter what age, sex, or if you have both legs or not, or how much you weigh going into it in order to be successful and advance. All it takes is a sincere devotion to Christ to follow the rules at that Level, and given enough experience *you will* get better as you increase in knowledge and experience within the discipline. I promise. Anyone can become great at fasting, and advance to whatever level they are led to by the Spirit, that is infinite within them. One is not bound by superior bodily performance, although it takes place by the body, but is freed by the performance of the Spirit inside that can do all things.

One last thing before I set you free to do some free writing in your *Journey Journal:* remember, I am just a guide to the art of fasting, not the last word. Jesus is the last word, and how his Spirit lives and moves and works in your life is what is true for you. If you feel prompted by the Holy Spirit to do something differently that what is outlined in these guidelines feel free to do so. For example, I have had to break the strict fasting rule before because it would have been extremely rude to the host who was serving me not to do so. There are occasions and some cases where Jesus would absolutely support your breaking the strict fasting rule. Only you will know when and what those are and that is also an important part of your individual journey with the Lord. I encourage you to write about these 'exceptions' because they can be very revealing and enlightening to your experience and spiritual growth overall. Make a note of it in your Personal DRL, of perhaps those times you have had to break or modify the strict fasting rule and why. Use these as opportunities to learn more about yourself, your lifestyle, your priorities, your motives, your values, and your love of Christ. You may or may not want to share these 'exceptions' or variations from the Rule with others. It is totally up to each individual. That is why this Bible Study is designed first and foremost to be done independently, by each person privately—between them and the Lord alone. Sure, it is nice to be able to get together or join a group session if you can, but, again, this is purely optional and not most important to the individual's spiritual growth or overall experience in fasting. The most important thing is that fasting is done in private, as were the Lord's instructions, and dedicated to the Father who sees everything done in private. That is how He knows it is done for His glory and not for the glory of man.

In the *Journey Journal* take the time to free write about possible favorite foods or ideas for meals and potential variations to drinks that you are brainstorming before the fast starts. What are some of your favorite go to foods and drinks, and how can you modify these to fit within the strict fasting rule? Come up with at least four potential, complete meals within the strict fasting rule. List some other food, (and drinks too), that you would like to try or incorporate into your Lenten fast. Keep it simple, simple, simple! Do not make it harder than it is! Think about it being easy and it will be. Also write about any initial thoughts, concerns, or feelings you have in regard to undertaking the fast.

JOURNEY JOURNAL

Therefore, I urge you, brothers, in view of God's mercy, to offer your bodies as living sacrifices, holy and pleasing to God—this is your spiritual act of worship. Do not conform any longer to the pattern of this world, but be transformed by the renewing of your mind. Then you will be able to test and approve what God's will is—his good, pleasing and perfect will.

—ROMANS 12:1-2

CHAPTER 2

SPIRITUAL GROWTH IS THE MAIN AIM

The main purpose of strict biblical fasting is spiritual growth and drawing closer to God through the Holy Spirit. Not perfection, but measurable progress in many areas of life involving the mind, body, and above all, Spirit is the goal. This is not a contemporary fad such as intermittent fasting or a popular diet. It is not a modern solution to the age-old problem of losing weight although that is one of the side effects and benefits of fasting proper. But I cannot emphasize enough that this is an ancient spiritual discipline that has been practiced for thousands of years, mainly by great spiritual leaders, common everyday Christians, prophets, and religious elders. The whole entire reason it is done is to bring one's soul into closer communion with God. One must be willing to surrender the body completely into His keeping for the duration of the fast and depend on Jesus in loving trust or else the overall direction could go astray. We must follow the Lord implicitly as the ultimate guide and example for fasting, looking to examples from the prophets as well, as is given us in the Holy Word. It is not a journey to be taken lightly because it does invoke the Holy Spirit, nor is it for the faint-hearted. Please, ensure that your motives and intentions of the heart are set on Jesus before committing yourself to this fast. Similar to double checking your luggage to make sure everything is packed correctly before getting on the plane for departure; reaffirm that your true motives in fasting are to grow spiritually upwards in Jesus Christ as the awesome perfecter of our faith.

All aboard the ship, we are about to leave the harbor, with the LORD God as the Captain! O, wait . . . some of our luggage is a little too heavy to bring on the celestial boat so we'll have to dive right in and start examining what we packed . . . yep, that is all our sins, character defects, personality characteristics of self-will, and bad habits galore! Phew! Those smelly socks are foul. It's high time to throw some of this excess weight overboard, or at least get it out in the light to access it for what it is here on the shore. One of the most important aspects of spiritual growth, as we will be focusing on in this Lenten fast, is fully acknowledging exactly what our sins are, recognizing them as sin which separates us further from God, and then purposefully handing them over to the One who came to earth to bear the burden for us. And then, voila! Abracadabra! He does completely and totally forgive us! Not only does he forgive us, he actually removes the sin from us so that we no longer carry it in our mind, body, or spirit! "For as high as the heavens are above the earth, so great is his steadfast love toward those who fear him; as far as the east is from the west, so far does he remove our transgressions from us" (Psalm 103: 11–12). Amen and Amen! Vanished into thin air are all those darkened weights we carry around which bind us in bonds of depression, anger, helplessness, fear and poverty. We must let go of these wrongful mistakes that we all make. Give it up to the Captain all ye merry folk who wish to travel much lighter when the real sun shines. There is nothing in those bulging bags that he hasn't already seen or doesn't know is there anyways. So, it is for your best interest and ultimate spiritual benefit to go ahead and admit (it needs be only between he and you) the nature of those sinful things so that you can get rid of them sooner rather than later. Many of the weekly Bible study activities are centered around spiritual acts in physical reality that represent us as sinners purposefully and completely asking Jesus to remove our sin from us, to forgive us. In order for him to give us the free grace of forgiveness, however, we have to acknowledge and be repentant (sorry for) the wrongful sin we are doing. That is some of the hard, yet necessary work, that calls each of us to partake in at Lent. From proper fasting, one honestly done for spiritual reasons and dedicated to His holiness, there abounds the fruit of Honesty, Self- Control, Discipline in all things, Integrity, Purity, Grace, Joy, Humility, and Selflessness.

TEMPTATIONS/SINS OF THE WORLD

Idolatry • Love of Money • Violence • Greed for Wealth • Fame Seeker • Neglect of Duties/Laziness • Addictions: to Alcohol (drunkenness) • Drugs (yes, that includes Marijuana) • Smoking/Tobacco Use • Stealing • Anger • Temper • Too Much Technology • Improper Use of Social Media •

Watching Bad Movies • Cursing • Abuse of others • Mistreatment of children • Overeating • Exploitation • Materialism • Sexual immorality • Modern Haste—have to always be busy • Overscheduling Time with none left for God • Overspending • Co-Dependence • Toxic relationships • Workaholic • Judgmental of others • Lying • Being Mean/Hateful to Others • Always having to be better than everyone else • Vanity • Unwillingness to Forgive others • Stressful/Anxious Lives

KEY VIRTUES CULTIVATED BY FASTING

Self-Control • Purity • Discipline • Strength • Gratitude • Health • Humility • Focus • Selflessness • Peace • Moderation • Love • Perseverance • Honesty • Patience • Courage • Faith • Beauty

DISCOVER THE KEYS OF LIFE BY CHRISTIAN FASTING

Simplify Life • True Contentment • Moderation in all things • Enjoy simple blessings • Live healthier, happier • More Time • Inner Peace • Spiritual Growth • Gives Eternal Life • Power to Change! • in the Moment

Personality Characteristics of Self-Will	Personality Characteristics of God's Will
Selfish and Self-Seeking	Selflessness
Dishonesty	Honesty
Fearful	Courageous
Rude	Considerate
Pride	Humble
Greedy	Helping Others
Lustful	Generous, Giving
Anger	Calm
Envy (covetousness)	Grateful
Laziness	Take Action/Active
Overindulgent (food, pleasures)	Self-Discipline
Impatient	Patient
Intolerant	Tolerance towards people
Resentment	Forgiveness
Hate	Love—genuine care for others

Harmful Acts	Good Deeds
Self-Pity	Responsible
Inflated Self-importance	Modesty
Doubt	Faith
Dissensions	Harmony
Argumentative	Peaceful
Foolishness	Wisdom
Egotistical	Meekness
Vanity	Modesty
Materialistic	Austere
Enmity	Joy
Negative thinking	Happiness
Self-righteous	Gracious
Conceited	Charity
Spoiled	Hard working/Industrious
Controlling	Free-Spirited
Mean	Kind
Rebellious	Service

GOD'S ATTRIBUTES TO MEDITATE ON

*Mercy • Goodness • Justice • Love • Truth • Creator • Powerful
Gracious • Wisdom • Holiness/Purity • Slow to Anger • Unchangeable*

CONSEQUENCES/RESULT OF SIN

Yelling • Cursing • Imprisonment • Rape • Fighting • Terrible Accidents • Despised • Unwanted Pregnancy • Loneliness • Costly Mistakes • Internal Warfare • Suffering • Harmful Acts • Major Setbacks • Loss of Job • Pain Death • Financial Ruin • Inconsequential • Remorse • Sickness • Divorce • Shame • Guilt • Lack of Health • Loss of Children • Ostracized from Society • Poverty • Destroyed relationships • Hell • Hate • Degradation of Character • Anger • Fear • Ignominy (public humiliation) • Helplessness • Diseased • Despised • Internal Warfare • Emptiness—life void of meaning • Isolation • Corruption of the Soul • Murder • Insanity • Ugliness • End up Alone • Bitter • Unhappy • Sadness • Suicide

Okay, now that we have all these great, long lists now the challenging part! Starting whenever you can and really focusing on these sins, temptations, and other virtues come Shrove Tuesday, will help open up the Spirit to also start working in you, in all of us. In fact, you can wait until Shrove Tuesday if you want to do this inventory, or if you feel prompted, do it whenever you like beforehand! The most important thing is to be very honest and transparent about what these are. Please, select *three* temptations or sins of the world from the first list and either circle or highlight them. Now, temptations face each of us everyday so that should be no problem, but understand that once we give in to the temptation that is sin. Maybe this temptation is one that you feel could become a danger or is threatening, and circle it. This promotes self-awareness and growth. Also carefully concentrate on which of those temptations may have already become a sin for you and circle it. Choose at least three, but if you feel prompted by the Spirit you may choose more. When Jesus was tempted by the Devil after his forty days of fasting he was so strong and pure that he was able to overcome it. This is one of the main purposes of fasting—to build up the strength and faith just as Jesus did while fasting—in order to overcome the temptations we face daily so that we may overcome them and not give in to sin.

Next, thoroughly review the list of Personality Characteristics of Self-Will versus the Personality Characteristics of God's Will. Much of Shrove Tuesday, the Tuesday before the beginning of Lent on Ash Wednesday, can be spent in deep and honest contemplation and reflection over what these personality tendencies could be. Even if they only come up every once in a great while, you could still put it down as one on your list to be improved upon. Please, go ahead and circle, highlight, or make a check next to *five* of these personality characteristics of self-will. Remember, these personality defects are not to be seen as bad defects or something to be ashamed of—everyone has them, just different ones—they are meant to be seen as an opportunity for ways to improve and grow in the knowledge of God's Will. Nobody has to see this personal "inventory" lists except you and "the Father of the heavenly lights, who does not change like shifting shadows" (James 1:17). It could be even something so simple as needing to get rid of clutter, and throw or donate old things away. That was and still is a problem that I battle, which is on my list . . . a difficulty throwing things away or donating them so that they mount up and become nonsense. It's terrible! So, out with the old junk—everything that is not readily usable or desirable—and in with the new! Or perhaps you need to work spiritually on forgiving someone in your immediate family or close friends and have true, complete reconciliation. Or perhaps you did something long ago in the past or are still harboring ill emotion from something that happened in the past that you need to let go of. You see, there is a whole spectrum of sins, various temptations and characteristics of self-will because I am trying to encompass as much of humanity as possible in the scope of this study. Some people have darker, harder problems and sins, and others lighter (but perhaps not easier ones to abolish). Keep that in mind throughout the study itself as it pertains to each unique individual and not like I am trying to vilify you in some negative way!

Along that vein, you are more than welcome to come up with your own, unique temptations, sins, problems, personality characteristics, and/or attributes of God. I am sure you do have individual things that you are working on, or specific problems that you need to hammer out, so seriously, feel free to come up with your own individual lists, or perhaps a few different additions or modifications to the suggested ones. I encourage you to do this! Go ahead and take your pen and neatly write in what those are or could be in the column beside the other sins given, personality characteristics of self-will, and attributes. Thus, you will have a deeply more meaningful study than if you could not find the right ones to fit your life. I tried to think of as many as I could, but the world is so big and people so complicated that there is no way I could include them all!

Also consider possible things that might not be obvious right away . . . perhaps something you did a long time ago that you never asked forgiveness for and that is why it still bugs you . . . a grievance you did against someone else that you should come clean about . . . a long-buried issue with a family member that needs reconciliation internally with God to move fully on . . . or perhaps somebody did something to you in childhood that you have never been able to truly forgive and still carry the weight of that which needs to be released. This is important "in bearing with one another and, if one has a complaint against another, forgiving each other; as the Lord has forgiven you, so you also must forgive" (Colossians 3: 13).

Lastly, study the section on God's attributes and choose *three* that seem to apply most to your life. Perhaps they are in ways that you have seen the LORD God active in your life recently or perhaps it is an attribute of his character that you want to become more full of. Go ahead and circle or highlight these three Godly attributes for later reference. We will come back to these pages later in the study for reference so be sure they are ready for when the time comes.

To end on a positive note, the point of all this morbid, brooding reflection on one's shortcomings is to be able to receive the ultimate, free gift of further grace granted us in the crucifixion and resurrection of Jesus the Christ and grow as believers. Yet we have to prepare ourselves in earnest, humble repentance to receive this glorious gift of redemption and purification from our sins, which he alone does through his blood. All we have to do, as sinners, is admit what these are, line them up on the scaffold, and literally give them over to the Messiah to take away on the cross. He always faithfully does this miraculous act of forgiveness to bring us eternally closer to God.

CHAPTER 3

PERSONAL DAILY RECORD LOG [DRL]

EXPLANATION OF THE DRL

The two most important aspects of the Personal Daily Record Log (DRL), is that it cultivates honesty and supplies personal motivation. It is the individual's factual record of their fast, recorded in detail each of the forty days they go without food all day long, and then what they eat for the humble meal allowed in the evening. The entries should be exact: first with the time eaten underlined and then underneath specifically what was eaten down to the detail! Be as precise and thorough as possible. All this establishes a nice, documentable account of integrity while fasting. Integrity is defined as doing what is right when nobody else can see. Well, the Lord sees and knows everything we do in private, so do him justice and be perfectly honest in the DRL. Anything and everything you eat should be meticulously recorded in the DRL for accountability purposes. It should also be a gratifying, satisfying part of the fasting process—daily logging this factual information. A great affirmation of the reality of what you are doing is witness by the DRL. It is a testimony of the journey undertaken to do this sacrificial self-offering to the Lord. Also make sure to write down at what time you eat (this should be only one time per day for the one meal, but of course, we are human)! Whenever I make a mistake and eat something at a time I shouldn't, or that consists of something I shouldn't have eaten, I put the symbol of a cross by it. You can observe this in my personal DRL that I have provided as an example which I hope will enlighten. Maybe don't see it as a mistake so much as room for growth and an opportunity to reflect back on and learn from. You can use whatever symbol you want to put next to any entries that may happen outside the strict fasting rules. Remember, these things are not meant to make you feel bad or that you did wrong, because that is not the case. It is an opportunity to be honest with yourself, and with the Lord, whom you are fasting for. See each entry and day as a new slate to become more honest, disciplined, steadfast, accountable, and ultimately more responsible for your overall spiritual growth in the faith.

Another main reason for the DRL is to hold each other accountable and provide motivation and inspiration at the bible studies—if and when they arise—where we can share these. That is why I encourage you to find a friend or someone else in the church to do this fast with you. It is not necessary, but it can be very helpful. The DRL is the one and only facet of the book that we can actually trade with someone else and share. The rest is private between the individual and the Lord. It is a great, easy record log that you can quickly bust out to show your trusted family and friends so they can see what you are doing for real! It is a wonderful way to share and show others the progress and reality of the forty-day fast you have undertaken, without revealing too much information that is just between you and your Creator. Give it all to God! Know that it is a living, breathing testimony of truth between you and him. Yes, it is nice to share it with others to receive motivation and secure more honesty and accountability along the journey, but ultimately it is meant for the Lord. Also, it should be noted that it is totally a personal choice whether or not you want to share your personal DRL log with anyone else. There will be a time allotted for this sharing, which should be very constructive and fun in the group bible studies, but if you are uncomfortable with it, that is perfectly fine. After all, it is designated for the Lord above anyone else and that is all that truly matters in the end. So don't feel bad if you do not want to share your DRL with anyone, that is totally acceptable and simply a personal choice.

There is a column for benefits you notice from fasting. These could be a broad spectrum of benefits ranging from emotions and spirituality to positive physical ones noticed. Write down two to three positive benefits you notice, or however many you wish, each day in the column as well as any side effects noticed. Refer to the example of my DRL as an example. These columns of how we feel and the benefits we notice as well as possible negative side effects sparks great group discussion while also helping to bring greater self awareness to the individual.

Come up with your own abbreviations for foods you tend to repeat a lot. There should be a lot of such foods because that is the nature of eating. So you ought to have quite a lot of certain foods that you consistently eat over and over again. Here is a list of example abbreviations I have used: WG for whole grain, PB for peanut butter, SC for sour cream, ND for non-dairy, etc. This just helps save space since the boxes are not very big to record everything... but maybe that is on purpose! Also, record any and all drinks you had throughout the day, but you do not have to record at what time for drinks, just food. There is no limit to drinks except of course, no dairy, no alcohol, and limited sugar. (See chapter 1 on instructions to review rules). Then, there is a funny Omega symbol in the drinks box each day. This represents the ideal amount of water that should be drunk each day: 91 ounces of water if you are a woman and 125 ounces of water if you are a man. Please, circle the horseshoe shaped omega symbol to show that you did, in fact, drink the full recommendation of water each day. Try to have the symbol circled every day of the fast! It is so very important to drink a lot of water while fasting and you will find yourself getting a lot thirstier than usual as your body cleanses itself of all the impurities and excess waste.

There is a place to record one's weight each day, but this is purely optional. I realize some people may not be comfortable with the weight thing, and I do not want this one detail to keep anyone from sharing at group or with trusted friends and family, so it is just an option if you want to do it. I like to do it because it is an awesome way of fact checking progress. After all, if you do not eat for periods of time and when you do it's within restricted limitations, you should lose weight. So, I find that keeping record of weight is a rewarding way to feel reassured that you are fasting properly as well as motivation overall. However, there can be no shame whatsoever regarding one's weight as long as it's done in a spirit of rightness. Even if many mistakes are made and someone snacks a lot there should be no shame because this is meant to be a positive, learning experience of personal growth in faith and food is actually quite beside the point. I know that sounds extremely confusing at this point, but once you are well into the fast and have begun to understand that food is just symbolic of a deeper, unseen spiritual reality, then it will make more sense. Retain the lessons learned and let go of any *mistakes* made, and give it all to the Lord. The most important thing to remember is that you are trying, and fasting is a difficult discipline. So, keep the spiritual growth moving forward no matter what, yet strive to be better, just as our Lord is perfect for our sake. Food is used as a means to get past the material into the spiritual realm where such liberating growth can be made.

Lastly, a capital X can be passionately made in the box of any day where one goes completely without any food at all. If this is your first time fasting you probably won't have too many of these, but if you want to challenge yourself, feel free to go for as many capital X's as possible. The end goal marked on the fasting treasure map.

PERSONAL STATEMENT OF DEDICATION

Before you begin the fast, on Ash Wednesday, please find some special time to say the following dedication out loud taken from the Dedication page: "I dedicate this Great Lent fast to the Lord, my Savior, who died on the cross for my sins so that I may have eternal life and peace with God."

JOURNEY JOURNAL

Free writing opportunity.

PERSONAL DAILY RECORD LOG [DRL]

Ω = Circle this Symbol each day you drink 64 oz. Water

	Any Food Consumed and At What Time	Benefits	Any Liquid drinks Taken throughout The Day	Possible Side Effects Felt
Day 1 Weight:			Ω	
Day 2 Weight:			Ω	
Day 3 Weight:			Ω	

Day 4 Weight:					Ω
Day 5 Weight:					Ω
Day 6 Weight:					Ω

Day 7 Weight:				Ω
Day 8 Weight:				Ω
Day 9 Weight:				Ω

Day 10 Weight:				Ω
Day 11 Weight:				Ω
Day 12 Weight:				Ω

Day 13 Weight:				Ω
Day 14 Weight:				Ω
Day 15 Weight:				Ω

Day 16 Weight:				Ω
Day 17 Weight:				Ω
Day 18 Weight:				Ω

Day 19 Weight:				Ω
Day 20 Weight:				Ω
Day 21 Weight:				Ω

Day 22 Weight:				Ω
Day 23 Weight:				Ω
Day 24 Weight:				Ω

Day 25 Weight:				Ω
Day 26 Weight:				Ω
Day 27 Weight:				Ω

Personal Daily Record Log [DRL]

Day 28 Weight:				Ω
Day 29 Weight:				Ω
Day 30 Weight:				Ω

| Day 31
Weight: | | | | Ω |
| Day 32
Weight: | | | | Ω |
| Day 33
Weight: | | | | Ω |

Day 34 Weight:				Ω
Day 35 Weight:				Ω
Day 36 Weight:				Ω

Day 37 Weight:				Ω
Day 38 Weight:				Ω
Day 39 Weight:				Ω

Day 40 Weight:					Ω

MY PERSONAL DRL FROM LENTEN FAST

(Example)

- Add your own abbreviations if necessary (ex. I have PB for peanut butter)
- This (+) symbol is to denote any time the fasting rule was broke

	Any Food Consumed and At What Time	Benefits	Any Liquid drinks Taken throughout The Day	Possible Side Effects Felt
Day 1 Weight: 131.4	X	Excitement Slow down Productive	- 3 cups coffee w/ creamer - 20oz. V8 - 8 oz. almond milk Ω	Loud growling stomach More Sensitive to Caffeine
Day 2 Weight: 129.4	X	Enhanced Prayer Compassion Focus	- 3 cups coffee w/ creamer - 20oz. green juice - 8 oz. almond milk Ω	Hungry Slightly Irritable

Day 3 Weight: 127.2	@ 6:15pm: - Bowl of split pea soup - ¼ baguette bread	Gratitude Selflessness Humility	- 2 cups coffee w/ creamer - 16 oz. almond milk Ω	
Day 4 Weight: 127.4	@ 6:15pm: - Bowl of beans w/ sprinkle cheese & SC - About 20 WG chips	Creative Self-Control Relaxed, no stress	- 3 cups coffee w/ creamer - 20oz. green juice - 8 oz. almond milk Ω	Slightly Irritable
Day 5 Weight: 129.0	X	Purity Vision Discipline	- 2 cups coffee w/ creamer - 20oz. green juice - 1 cup hot cider Ω	Fatigue
Day 6 Weight: 127.8	X	Strength Faith Confidence Good Will	- 2 cups coffee w/ creamer - 1 cup hot cider - 20oz. green juice - 10 oz. almond milk Chai Ω	Hungry

Personal Daily Record Log [DRL] 45

Day 7 Weight: 125.6	@6:20pm: - Bowl lentil soup - ¼ baguette - 2 mini muffins +	Humility Grace Confidence	- 2 cups coffee w/ creamer - 1 cup hot cider - 20oz. green juice - 10 oz. almond milk Chai	Light-headedness
Day 8 Weight: 127.2	@6:15pm: - WG pasta and pesto - few banana chips - few chips and SC - 1 Tbsp. PB, honey - Sourdough bread	Faith Concentration Happiness Love	- 2 cups coffee w/ creamer - 1 cup hot cider - 10 oz. almond milk Chai Ω	Slightly Irritable
Day 9 Weight: 127.0	X	Gratitude Happiness Focus	- 3 cups coffee w/ creamer - 1 cup hot cider - 20 oz. V8 Ω	
Day 10 Weight: 125.4	@ 6:15pm: - bowl of beans w/ sprinkle cheese & SC -WG Chips -5 Tbsp. PB & honey - 2 graham crackers - 6 bites of cake +	Peace Gratitude Faith	- 2 cups coffee w/ creamer - 1 cup hot cider - 20 oz. V8 Ω	Light Headedness

Day 11 Weight: 127.4	X	Discipline Clarity Peace	- 3 cups coffee w/ creamer - 1 cup hot cider - 20 oz. V8 Ω	
Day 12 Weight: 125.2	@ 6:30pm: - Bowl minestrone w/ sprinkle cheese & SC - 2 pieces bread - Baked potato w/ SC - 4 Tbsp. PB & honey	Patience Endurance Self-Control	- 2 cups coffee w/ creamer - 1 cup hot cider - 20 oz. V8 Ω	Stomach cramps
Day 13 Weight: 127.0	@ 6:30pm: - Bowl split pea soup - 2 pieces bread - 6 Tbsp. PB & honey	Peace Discipline Love	- 2 cups coffee w/ creamer - 1 cup hot cider - 20 oz. V8 Ω	
Day 14 Weight: 127.8	X	Self-Control Love Faith	- 3 cups coffee w/ creamer - 1 cup hot cider - 20 oz. V8 Ω	
Day 15 Weight: 125.2	@ 6:15pm: - Bowl veg. barley soup - 2 pieces bread - 7 Tbsp. PB & Honey	Faith Obedience Serenity	- 2 cups coffee w/ creamer - 20 oz. green juice - 1 cup hot cider - 20 oz. V8 Ω	Headache

Day 16 Weight: 126.6	@ 6:15pm: - Vegetable pakora - Indian lentil curry - Naan bread - Pistachio Ice cream + - Basmati rice	Love Joy Faith	- 2 cups coffee w/ creamer - Indian tea - 16 oz. soy chai Ω	
Day 17 Weight: 127.5	X	Peace Self-control Contentment	—2 cups coffee w/ creamer - 16oz. soy chai - 1 cup hot cider - 20 oz. V8 Ω	
Day 18 Weight: 126.6	@ 6:15pm: - Bowl of beans w/ sprinkle cheese & SC - WG Chips - Little piece of cake + @10:15pm & 12:15am: 2 TBSP PB & Honey +	Wisdom Serenity Happiness	- 3 cups coffee w/ creamer - 16 oz. green juice - 1 cup hot cider Ω	Little groggy in the morning
Day 19 Weight: 127.0	@ 7:15pm: - Bowl of pesto pasta - 3 TBSP. PB & Honey	Joy Self-control Gratitude	- 2 cups coffee w/ creamer - 12oz. soy chai Ω	

Day 20 Weight: 127.0	@ 6:15pm: - Bowl of beans w/ sprinkle cheese & SC - WG Chips	Love Hope Peace	- 2 cups coffee w/ ceamer - 16oz. soy chai - 20 oz. V8 Ω	
Day 21 Weight 127.0:	± @ 4:15pm: - Vegetable Pakora - Chickpeas masala - Vegetable curry - Garlic Naan bread	Discipline Peace Focus	- 2 cups coffee w/ creamer - 16oz. Chai Ω	
Day 22 Weight: 125.8	@ 6:00pm: - Bowl of Lentil soup w/ dallop SC - 2 pieces of bread & butter - ½ cup of beets	Productivity Contentment Grace	- 2 cups coffee w/ creamer - 16 oz. coconut milk Chai - 1 cup hot cider Ω	Irritability Headache
Day 23 Weight: 125.8	@ 6:30pm: - Bowl of soup w/sprinkle cheese, SC - 2 pieces fresh baked bread w/ butter - 6 Tbsp. PB & honey	Calm Love Faith Self-control	- 3 cups coffee w/ creamer - 1 cup veg. broth - 1 cup hot cider - 20 oz. V8 Ω	Extra Thirsty

Day 24 Weight: 127.2	@ 6:30pm: - Bowl of soup w/sprinkle cheese, SC - 2 pieces fresh baked bread w/ butter - 6 Tbsp. PB & honey	Faith Purity Love	- 3 cups coffee w/ creamer - 1 cup hot cider - 20 oz. V8 Ω	
Day 25 Weight: 126.8	@ 6:30pm: - 2 pieces of bread w/ butter - 5 Tbsp. PB & honey - Few Doritos chips	Joy Serenity Self-control	- 3 cups coffee w/ creamer - 1 cup hot cider - 20 oz. V8 Ω	Irritable
Day 26 Weight: 127.2	@ 6:30pm: - Bowl of Lentils - 5 Tbsp. PB & honey - 2 pieces fresh bread w/ butter	Peace Gratitude Perseverance	- 2 cups coffee w/ creamer - 1 cup hot cider - 20 oz. V8 Ω	Groggy
Day 27 Weight: 126.4	@ 6:30pm: - Half Veggie Sub - Oatmeal cookie	Happiness Focus Time	- 2 cups coffee w/ creamer - 1 cup hot cider - 20 oz. V8 Ω	
Day 28 Weight: 126.4	@ 5:30pm: - Half Veggie Sub - Oatmeal cookie - ¼ bean burrito	Joy Generosity Responsibility	- 2 cups coffee w/ creamer - 1 cup hot cider - 12 oz. Soy Latte	Ω

Day 29 Weight: 126.6	@ 6:00pm: - Bowl curried lentils - 2 pieces sourdough bread w/ butter - 5 Tbsp. PB & honey	Wisdom Patience Peace	- 3 cups coffee w/ creamer - 1 cup hot cider - 20 oz. V8	Slight Headache Ω
Day 30 Weight: 127.0	@ 6:00pm: - Bowl of beans w/ sprinkle cheese, SC - WG chips - 5 T PB & honey	Service Humility Honesty	- 2 cups coffee w/ creamer - 1 cup hot cider	Cold Ω
Day 31 Weight: 127.2	@ 6:15pm: - Bowl of Veg. Soup - 2 pieces Sourdough bread w/ butter - 5 T PB & honey + @ 12:15am +: - 5 Tbsp. PB & honey	Peace Productive Hope	- 2 cups coffee w/ creamer - 1 cup hot cider - 20 oz. V8	Sensitive to Cold Ω
Day 32 Weight: 128.4	@ 6:15pm: - Bowl of Veg. Lentils - 2 pieces Sourdough bread w/ butter - 5 T PB & honey	Love Hope Faith	- 3 cups coffee w/ creamer - 1 cup hot cider - 20 oz. green juice	Ω

Day 33 Weight: 127.8	@ 6:15pm: - Bowl of beans w/ sprinkle cheese & SC - 2 pieces Sourdough bread w/ butter - 5 T PB & honey	Joy Purity Patience Self-Control	- 3 cups coffee w/ creamer - 1 cup hot cider - 20 oz. green juice	Fatigue Ω
Day 34 Weight: 126.8	@ 6:30pm: - Bowl of split pea soul w/ SC - 2 pieces Sourdough bread w/ butter - 5 T PB & honey	Peace Discipline Purity	- 2 cups coffee w/ creamer - 1 cup hot cider - 20 oz. green juice	Ω
Day 35 Weight: 127.2	@ 9:00pm: - Bowl Granola w/ almond milk - 5 T PB & honey	Love Compassion Honesty	- 3 cups coffee w/ creamer - 1 cup hot cider - 20 oz. V8/ green juice	Ω
Day 36 Weight: 126.8	@ 6:30pm: - Bowl of Lentils - 2 pieces Sourdough bread w/ butter - 5 T PB & honey	Faith Compassion Wisdom	- 3 cups coffee w/ creamer - 12 oz. soy milk chai - 20 oz. green juice	Ω
Day 37 Weight: 126.6	@ 5:15pm: - 2 pancakes w/ butter & syrup - 5 T PB & honey	Courage Purpose Grace	- 3 cups coffee w/ creamer - 1 cup hot tea	Ω

Day 38 Weight: 127.2	@ 6:30pm: - Bowl of Golden lentils - 2 pieces Sourdough bread w/ butter - 5 T PB & honey	Love Humility Discipline	- 3 cups coffee w/ creamer - 1 cup hot cider - 20 oz. green juice	Ω
Day 39 Weight: 126.5	@ 6:30pm: - Bowl of black bean soup - 2 pieces Sourdough bread w/ butter - 5 T PB & honey	Love Humility Service	- 3 cups coffee w/ creamer - 1 cup hot cider - 20 oz. green juice	Ω
Day 40 Weight: 126.2	@ 6:30pm: - 2 Spinach Enchiladas - Chips and salsa - Rice and beans	Joy Humility Meekness	- 2 cups coffee w/ creamer - 16 oz. Horschata (Mexican drink)	Ω

CHAPTER 4

ON MEDITATION

Similar to the ancient spiritual discipline of fasting, meditation is another lost and neglected form of worship from the past that we can benefit greatly from. I believe the two disciplines go hand and hand, along with prayer. Why should we Christians let the Buddhists and Eastern religions have all the fun with meditation? Is not this miraculous, healing, spiritual way of communing with God prescribed and recorded for its truth throughout all of Holy Scripture? So, why do we see it being practiced mostly by Buddhists, monks, and other Eastern religions? Meditation is a traditional, purely Christian form of seeking, communing, and understanding the one true God better. Practiced as a way of life by early Christians and exulted by the early Church, meditation is an eternal wellspring of knowing Jesus better intimately. It is at the very roots of Christianity itself! It is a most ancient form of biblical worship dating back to Genesis, being practiced by many, if not most, of the Old Testament prophets, and flows pervasively through the Psalms. Beginning in Genesis: "Isaac went out to the field one evening to *meditate*, and as he looked up, he saw camels approaching" (Genesis 24:63). God's people were meditating as far back as Genesis, and it did not stop there! Does that not immortally establish meditation at the roots of Christianity and Christianity in the roots of meditation? Meditation should be more part of the Christian lifestyle, as it is an incredible way of life. In Joshua the Word of God says; "Keep this Book of the Law always on your lips; *meditate* on it day and night, so that you may be careful to do everything written in it. Then you will be prosperous and successful" (Joshua 1:8).

So, similar to fasting, what happened to this most sacred Christian form of worship of the One true Creator? Unfortunately, this Old World strategy for slowing down to daily connect with our Higher Power has been forgotten, neglected, and misunderstood in this hectic, busy New World of technology. Everyone is so busy on computers, darting or driving here or there and ordering stuff on Amazon that these old ways of living in the spiritual world are quite unsavory. To sit down to meditate, contemplate, and think about the Lord Almighty and his Word does not quite fit into most modern day American schedules (or thinkers). That is why it is important to put the time aside to do it anyways, which is what this Lent Fasting Bible Study prescribes: setting aside 10 minutes to meditate each day for your great, great benefit.

The benefits and rewards are immense that come from meditation. The serenity and peace of God surround those that meditate regularly. An unprecedented calm enters the mind that can be returned to at any moment needed. When practiced diligently for at least ten to fifteen minutes a day, (I have been doing thirty minutes to an hour a day for nearly three years now), an unfathomably deep peace encompasses the being with an unshakable permanence. If at any time you need to return to this wonderful calming space—free of stress, free of anxiety, worry, or fear—you can easily do so with more and more practice. It does take putting in the time and actually doing it to improve and reap the benefits. For instance, I use the spiritual skills and weapons learned and gained from meditation all the time: in a heated disagreement with my spouse I return to that meditative calm in abundance and can hold the angry words and keep my voice down; in dealing with two boys under age five I can have enough faith and love of the Lord to be in touch with them anew, fresh in meditation everyday to get through the hard times. At night sometimes when I cannot fall asleep, I go into meditation mode and can fall asleep quickly whereas before I would have lost five more hours of sleep! In fact, there actually a lot of Scripture versus related directly to meditation at night, which is interesting. For instance it says, "Let me remember my song in the night; let me *meditate* in my heart" (Psalm 77:6). It's absolutely amazing how the power of meditation can and will manifest itself into the rest of your personal life and aid you in times of need, to get you through the storm. Even in line, waiting at the bank, or next to angry customers, you can instantly warp into your collected space of meditation and stay cool through it all!

So, how do you meditate? A beautiful description is given to us in the Holy Word: "I remember the days of old; I *meditate* on all that you have done; I ponder the work of your hands. I stretch out my hands to you; my soul thirsts for you like a parched land" (Psalm 143: 5–6). Well, I could go on and on for pages and pages with instructions and tips of shared experience on how to do it, but I will try to keep it short for your reading pleasure. Here in scripture we are not only given a visual image of a fellow believer stretching out their hands in meditation of the Most High, but also instructions and tips for how to do it. Synonyms of meditation in God's Holy Word can be interchangeable with *remember, ponder, think, wait, reflect, sit still,* and a few more unlisted here. Whenever you come across one of these verbs defining an activity of the mind, it relates to the function and purpose of Christian meditation. Still further, the purpose of meditation is to (as the Psalm shows) *remember* the miraculous deeds God has done from the beginning, as well as *ponder* His mighty works. Meditation is a way of thinking, as we actively reflect on God's miraculous power, character, love, and mighty deeds from all time recorded in his Word. That is why it is most helpful to have a scripture verse before you in meditation to come back to—I have provided one for most days—or simply pick one out that is pertinent to your life or as you are prompted to do. Then, with the Scripture actually visible nearby where you are sitting, find solace and refuge in *pondering, remembering, meditating, thinking,* on the truth and love that it conveys from the Father. Let its significance in your daily life soak through your thought processes and provide clarity, direction, and peace.

First, find a comfortable place to sit—preferably outside if it is nice enough, or on a cushioned seat inside if it is not nice enough to be outdoors. A strong back support is essential, as we are going to be sitting for a while, with our legs either cross-legged or as they would normally be while seated. Reach up tall and upright through the spine as you make a solid, right angle with your body. The bottom of the sacrum, or the tailbone, should be squarely drawn up under you, while the seat bones touch down, forming a triangle at the base of the seat, comfortably to retain posture as we sit. Now, you can let the tops of your hands rest at ease anywhere on your legs while tucking the elbows in at the side of the rib cage, or you can raise them in the air. If you raise them in the air, still, keep your elbows in by your sides. Hands may be outstretched in a gesture of open praise. This illustration of hands outstretched is given many times in the Psalms.

Once you feel comfortable in your seated position focus on relaxing every square inch of your body and entering into a great space of peace, serenity, and calm with the Lord. Relax your jaw, your feet, your face, literally every inch of flesh on your frame, and let go of all thoughts, stress, and tension as you surrender and submit to the Lord, giving him this time of worship. Let the mind quiet as you breathe deeply in and out through the nose. If you start to have a distracting thought or stress come up, purposefully and firmly return to your breath and focus on retaining that sense of purity until the calming peace and serenity returns. You should keep all thoughts out, except the higher forms of meditations on the Lord of the spiritual kind. This will bring the mind onto an elevated thought-plane where better thinking actually happens anyways, so it is not any loss to just find your brain's on/off switch and shut off that interfering, inferior slew of thoughts that are not helpful. Once you have kind of located the on and off switch to where thoughts stem from in the brain, it will behoove you greatly so that you can quickly identify it and turn it back off if the thoughts come back.

Next, allow your body to become completely still. This is the main, defining feature of meditation—the unmoving, statuesque essence of the form as it contemplates God. Allow yourself to just be, whatever that means. We are all diverse, amazing human *beings*, so let us practice *being* in God's presence through prayer and meditating on God's Word. That is what meditation encourages us to do: slow down and just allow ourselves to be for a little while with God each day. If you start to drift away, have a favorite Scripture handy—or look to one of the one's I have provided for these forty days on meditation—to help ground the mind in the present and breathe on. There is a massive wealth of resources inside you—the wellspring of Life in Jesus, the living water—that meditation on the Word awakens. Let his amazing love, joy, healing tranquility, and endless truth wash over you. Connect with the Kingdom of Heaven within, for it exists inside you, as meditation brings you closer to the resurrected Savior. The daily walk of faith grows intimately closer with the Lord as we open our hearts and surrender our Spirits to the One who abides in the Father, and we in him, and he in us, in the great mystery of being. Seek out this Oneness that Jesus talks about time and again throughout Scripture, and feel his Spirit moving in you. Make space, room, and time for the power to work and manifest itself in phenomenal spiritual growth in everyday, private life. Our everyday walk with the Lord as *everyday Christians* is strengthened in the best ways of faith, hope, and love of our God as we learn to practice these ancient ways whenever and wherever we are. Nothing can stand in the way of connecting with the Spirit of the Lord as he lives in each of us in the Body of Christ as we enter into that peaceful meditative space and practice these good, old ways. Devote ten minutes each of these forty days, (and more if you want), to tapping into the power of Jesus Christ who lives and reigns inside of you and better grasp and feel what that means!

Another helpful strategy of meditation is spiritual visualization. Instead of thoughts, open your mind's cortex to the visionary realm and be comforted by the results. Imagine as you meditate all things of permanent, eternal value. All the unmoving structures of the earth: The trees, statues, rocks, homes, stone buildings, mountains and now... you! Visualize yourself as a statue—unmoving, so perfectly still—becoming evermore a part of the scene of eternal reality, the Natural, Old World that God made. Open all your senses and try hard to stay focused to retain Purity without thought or common distraction. Listen to the chirping birds and the sounds around. Smell the grass or recent rain. If inside, perhaps play a nature sounds tape to help stay in tune with this perfectly still, relaxed, pure state of being. Practice just being fully awake. True wakefulness and a sense of readiness is a perfect way to be for meditation. Find reassurance in your eyes being eyes—blinking or closed—your ears being ears, your nose being a nose, your feet being feet, your hair just being hair, and so on and so forth ad infinitum. Meditation is truly, at essence, just being alive. One cannot mess it up! Just let every piece and member of yourself be and find enduring gratification in this. Listen to your heartbeat, tune into the breath. Simply sit there and be alive and keep distracting thoughts out that would interfere with coming into that lively space of being alive. I find being outside facilitates in every way the best modes of meditation. Plus, it is more enjoyable and even pleasurable if you are in the sun and just relaxing, being yourself. Once you have come into that immovable, perfectly still form; simply assume that you are meditating because you are! There is no magic trick, or test you have to pass. All you have to do is be totally still, keep distracting thoughts out of your head, breathe, and be content with however you are in the moment. Then, let yourself go... wherever the Spirit takes you. You may be filled with compassion, with joy, with love, with further peace, with healing balm, with gratitude, with contentment, with wonder, with excitement. Just let yourself be in whatever space the Spirit shows himself and be content.

My absolute favorite Scripture to meditate on is the one about living stones: "As you come to him, a living stone rejected by men but in the sight of God chosen and precious, you yourselves like living stones are being built up as a spiritual house, to be a holy priesthood, to offer spiritual sacrifices acceptable to God through Jesus Christ" (1 Peter 2: 4–5). Jesus is the living stone, the Foundation of our Faith—the Rock that we put all of our faith, trust, and life in. He is all that is unchangeable, permanent, eternal, and true. Everything we believe in or do is based on the reality that He lives. He exists at the right hand of the Father. Yet, we also are being built up as similar *living stones* into a spiritual house. Therefore, I want you to picture yourself as a *living stone* and what that would look like. I find this metaphor extremely apt in helping me meditate to the best of my ability. Actually picture your arms, your crossed-legs, your hands, your neck, your head, as stone, like a sculpture. Visualize your body as being solid rock. What are some ways to describe stone or rock? Some synonyms for starters are hard, heavy, solid, impenetrable, strong, resilient, permanent, eternal, unmoving, and tough. Even reflect on this list of adjectives beforehand and come up with some more on your own to help bring you into that state of being *living stones*. Imagine your bodies as you meditate as hard, dense, solid granite, or marble, or whatever stony material of your choice. Become the Rock, more like Jesus, our Redeemer. So still, so calm, so smooth, so eternal are stones and so are we. Now, picture the stoniness of your limbs and bodies as living, breathing vessels of truth. For although the stony rocks of our meditating bodies remain still and entirely unmoving as stones, they are living and breathing entities all the while. Envision the blood, the breath, the muscles; cells dividing and pulsing underneath and through the solid stones. Two exact opposites exquisitely coupled into eternity together—stones and life. Stones are not living! They do not breathe or move! But breathed into by the Holy Spirit they do! Meditation is an act of the heart. It is an acceptable form of worship to God in which we give ourselves, our pure bodies as a spiritual offering. In meditation we give our time, ourselves, and place our focus on the keeper of eternity. It is a sacred time to dwell and commune with the Lord alone.

The same is true of trees. Think of how long trees remain planted in one place in the earth—how many centuries sometimes—how unmoving ancient, and permanent as statues or stones are trees; yet living, breathing organisms all the while. Why do we humans find the need to move so much? Why must we constantly propel ourselves, and everyone around us into a frenzy of activity to feel accomplishment or like we have lived? Is it not a great accomplishment or wonder for the tree to stay rooted to the same square foot of land for a hundred years? Could we ever even hope or dare to do such a thing? What about our homes? Is it not a great accomplishment to stay in the same place and live abundantly year after year? The Word of God encourages us to slow down and practice the still, unmoving ancient worship of meditation. Envision the trees, the blueness of the sky, the sun, the rocks around, and all the creation God has made in this ultimate reality as you become One with all that is. Connect and commune with the Holy Spirit as you abide in Jesus. He abides in the Father and in us and we are healed, and made whole. Return to the breath, the powerful spirit of meditation, and God's Word, whenever or wherever you may need to at any time during the rest of your days and feel a comforting return to all that is eternal. The more you practice meditation the better you will get, so enjoy learning and adapting this wonderful form of praise and glorifying God in our bodily temples for a richly enhanced spiritual life. Sink further into the holy, ancient practice each day for the forty days, and take it with you hopefully for the future beyond! It is a true wellspring of eternal life that has El Roi at the Foundation.

May these words of my mouth and this meditation of my heart be pleasing in your sight, LORD, my Rock and my Redeemer.

PSALM 19:14

My mouth will speak words of wisdom; the meditation of my heart will give you understanding.

PSALM 49:3

CHAPTER 5

ON PRAYER

Prayer is one of my favorite words in the English dictionary. I love the active ending that has been almost entirely overlooked. Look at these other verbs: swimmer, skier, runner, mother, father, producer, writer, teacher, horseback-rider, lover, reader, singer, caller, soccer player, speaker, and lastly prayer. All of these activities inherently encompass the one who does the sublime activity in the word itself—as seen in the 'er' ending. The one who swims, the one who runs, the one who plays a sport, the one who sings, the one who rides a horse, the one who loves, ad infinitum. There is a human recognition in the word itself that describes the one who does it. Thus, the word prayer itself encompasses all the believers who do this heavenly worship unto God, as the one who prays. We as believers are not left out of the word prayer. It is an *active* spiritual activity that takes believers to do. I think sometimes the holy grail of prayer is often seen as a stagnant, passive component of worship. However, this is not the case at all. To pray properly and be heard on high requires active engagement of the spirit. Similar to fasting, it is a spiritual activity that requires action on behalf of the prayer—the one who prays. "And when you stand praying, if you hold anything against anyone, forgive him, so that your Father in heaven may forgive your sins" (Mark 11: 25).

Fasting and prayer are intertwined eternally throughout scripture. Almost like peanuts and cracker jacks, or black and white, or pancakes and syrup, fasting and prayer is an irreversibly perfect combination. You cannot have one without the other, or it simply would not be complete! There would always be something lacking if you performed fasting without prayer, although it is not the same way in reverse . . . you can, of course, pray without fasting. That is an important differentiation to make. So, whenever you are fasting, especially for long periods of time such as forty days, prayer should always be a central part of your daily routine. Prayer is one of the pillars supporting a biblical fast that honors and glorifies God. Studying the Word of God regularly and meditation are the two other pillars I consider it absolutely necessary to fasting really well. However, prayer is much more important than meditation.

One of the best examples we have from Scripture of the ideal combination of fasting and prayer is with Anna the prophetess: "And there was a prophetess, Anna, the daughter of Phanuel, of the tribe of Asher. She was advanced in years, having lived with her husband seven years from when she was a virgin, and then as a widow until eighty-four. She did not depart from the temple, worshiping with fasting and prayer night and day" (Luke 2: 36–38). Notice how it does not say that she worshiped in the temple with just fasting alone, or with just praying by itself. Rather, Anna worshiped with both these eternal, ancient ways anointed biblically together in unison. The two forms of worship are interlinked immortally, and designated as being done together by the Word of God itself. There is no substitute for prayer while fasting. So, we also should follow the example of Anna the prophetess in the Bible as we fast biblically for the Lord. If it seems hard at times, remember Anna, and the stalwart soul she was. She hungered for God and showed her strong emotions of being separated from him by constantly, everyday, worshiping him with fasting and praying in the temple. "For Anna that yearning meant a life of *fasting* and praying, decade after decade—probably sixty years since her husband died—as she ministered in the temple."[1]

The main reason for fasting to begin with is to increase the power of prayer. Therefore, it should be seen as a pillar to prayer itself, and not the other way around. When you are in the spirit of fasting you are drawing so much closer to God, and this helps make your prayers that much more poignant. "Fasting is designed to make prayer mount up as on eagles' wings. It is intended to usher the supplicant into the audience chamber of the King and to extend to him the golden scepter. It may be expected to drive back the oppressing powers of darkness and loosen those powers' hold on the prayer objective. It is calculated to give an edge to a person's intercessions and power to their petitions. Heaven is ready to bend its ear to listen when someone prays with fasting."[2] That is why when someone really wants some-

---

1. Piper, *Hunger for God*, 83.
2. Wallis, *God's Chosen Fast*, 62.

thing from God, or is in a desperate plight or situation or problem, they pray with fasting to be heard that much more powerfully by the author of the universe. It is like taking two elemental forces and when you put them together a magical reaction takes place, exploding into a trillion cosmic particles. There is a supernatural power in each of these ancient forms of worship, so when they are combined it doubles the divine potential. Picture a bright blue ray emanating from a sword in the east, and a green ray illuminating the sword in the west, and when they mystically clash—as with fasting and prayer—a bright, white light shoots up to the heavens in a huge beam! There is so much untapped power in the combination of prayer with fasting that is only up to the individual to discover the wealth of resources inside each of us—in the Kingdom of Heaven within.

What is prayer after all but an ongoing communication with Jesus? It is a way of talking to the greatest Counselor about what is going on in our spiritual life—what we need, what others need, what we care about, what we want to see happen, expressing where we are at emotionally, being fully understood by the Creator, asking for specific requests, praising Him in many ways—are all aspects of prayer. Praying is done corporately, as a congregation at church, and should also be done privately by believers in the body of Christ on a daily basis. Everyone is probably slightly different in the way they pray. Personally, I like to say the prayer out loud, similar to how prayers are audible in church or Bible study. Of course, I usually don't like to be in the middle of the park or grocery market when I pray because it would look as though I were crazy, talking to myself! Meditation and prayer are a prescribed component to each of the forty days of fasting, however, the amount of time you spend in each may vary. The ten minutes recommended for each form of worship is a suggestion or guideline that is open to flexibility. Maybe you spend fifteen minutes meditating and five minutes in prayer. Or perhaps you prefer to spend most of the time praying one day on a difficult issue and leave only five minutes for meditation. Truly, how you do this is entirely up to you; I have merely provided a guideline. Also, on a personal note, I find that meditating first helps elevate my thought-plane to prepare me better for prayer. In other words, meditation is a little easier to get into, and helps me prepare my mind and heart for prayer. Meditation quiets the thoughts, puts me in a space of purity, and in touch with the spiritual realm where Christ abides.

This study is aimed at helping Christians incorporate prayer into their daily lives, strengthening their faith and personal relationship with the Lord. Fasting helps strengthen the willingness of one to pray because it is also an everyday spiritual discipline that must be adapted. Fasting strengthens, encourages, and facilitates prayer and vice versa. The two are soul mates and should be done with committed vigilance. An author I absolutely adore is Susan Gregory who wrote *The Daniel Fast*. I learned so much from reading her experience with imitating the twenty-one day fast of the prophet Daniel. The power of prayer in regards to fasting was so important that she wrote the following to those entering the Daniel Fast: "Even now begin praying to your Father and ask Him to bless you. Open your heart to Him so that He will show you truths that He wants you to know. Dedicate yourself and the fast to Him. And listen for His words as you purpose to position yourself humbly before your Lord. This is the most important step as you prepare for your fast."[3] Therefore, let us go forth with happy, humble hearts ready to kneel down and pray before the Lord while fasting these forty days. Raise your voice and unearth the power within made strong by practicing these ancient ways! Allow the transformation that unfolds as the words take root in heaven and manifest in real life by the spirit.

Below is a list of world problems and specific people to pray for that can be done corporately in the group Bible study, or on your own privately. Circle at least three problems to pray for from the list. Feel free to once again add any other World problems that you find pertinent today to the list. Unfortunately, the list may get quite long as we live in very distressing, tumultuous modern times. Also, create your own personal list of people or specific things to pray for to refer back to continually throughout the forty-days. O, and don't forget yourself!

<u>World Problems</u>   <u>Prayers for Specific People / Other Problems</u>
War Invasions
Covid-19 wake
Human Trafficking
World Hunger
Poverty
Energy Crisis
Violence
Racism
Abortion
Political Strife
Child Abuse
Hatred/Divisions Amongst People

---

3. Gregory, *The Daniel Fast*, 58.

LITTLE POCKET PRAYER SCROLLS

Happy praying! Here is a little helpful aid that I like to use each day, or sometimes week, for keeping track of my prayers. I have found that by filling in these prayer scrolls each week and keeping it on my person all day long helps make my days go better. It creates kind of a cross connection between prayer and meditation where I am constantly reminded of what is in the forefront of my mind, certain needs and requests for the Lord that I have, and also what I am most grateful for. It also helps keep my prayer requests specific and therefore effective. I am able to pray for certain people and world problems better because I actually remember them! It may sound silly but it's the truth. It is the same way for me at the grocery store . . . if I don't write it down I forget it . . . it's actually kind of scary how I can forget things from one second to the next. I kind of remind myself of Dory in Little Nemo! So, try to do these prayer scrolls each week of the seven weeks of fasting to help keep focused and effective in prayer, if you want. This method can also help during your prayer time each day to refer back to if you need. It also comes in handy if you are talking to someone in passing who has a problem they need prayed for that you can immediately add to your list so you do not forget it later.

Anyways, these prayer scrolls are truly very helpful in enhancing and building up prayer life, so I have provided you with an example one and then left the rest blank so that you can just rip out this page and cut them out to use. When you run out, just make your own using small, similar sized paper. Receipts work great, as do business cards or colorful sticky notes are awesome because you can have plenty of room to write out your prayer requests and praises and then fold it in half and carry it easily anywhere! Besides the prayers and praises you would like to lift up spiritually to the Lord that particular day, try choosing two virtues from the list found on page nineteen under *Key Virtues Cultivated by Fasting* and write them on either side of the cross at the top of your scroll for each day. These can be any virtues that you feel filled with, or wanting to cultivate more, or maybe have been lacking lately and need to work on. Carrying these with you can help you be aware of these different spiritual sides of yourself; either rejoicing in their overflow of abundance on a particular day or so as to serve as a reminder for inspiration to grow in these ways.

Again, this is what works for me, so I have simply provided it for you if it helps. If it doesn't fit your style, that's totally fine, don't do it. It's completely an optional activity meant to be fun, not unnecessary work. The prayer scrolls are just meant to be a further helpful aid and if it doesn't work for you that's perfectly okay. I find these prayer scrolls very powerful in keeping me focused on exact people, problems, things, and finding balance in it all throughout the day. But that is just me; everyone is so individual in the way they pray, so you need to decide if this is conducive to prayer for you or not. It is almost like setting a goal and then carrying it with you, on your person, in your heart, all day long so that you can constantly return to it to see how you are doing in reaching your goal. Sometimes I put my scroll in jewelry like a big shell necklace, or through a hole in the link of a chain on a bracelet. Keep it fun and spiritual no matter what!

Ex. Prayers: Hope + Faith
1. Positive outcome on Shirley's blood tests
Reconciliation for cousin with my aunt
Peace treaty between Putin and Zelensky
For my oldest son's ankle to get better for track
Praise:
1. The approach of summer and days getting nicer
2. My husband's new job that includes benefits
3. Three Healthy children

Prayers:
1.
2.
3.
4.
Praise:
1.
2.
3.

Do not be anxious about anything, but in everything, by prayer and petition, with thanksgiving, present your request to God.

PHILIPPIANS 4:6-7

Prayers:+
1.
2.
3.
4.
Prayers:+
1.
2.

3.
4.
Praise:
1.
2.
3.

But when you pray, go into your room, close the door and pray to your Father, who is unseen. Then your Father, who sees what is done in secret, will reward you. And when you pray, do not keep on babbling like pagans, for they think they will be heard because of their many words. Do not be like them, for your Father knows what you need before you ask him.

MATTHEW 6:6–8

Prayers:+
1.
2.
3.
4.
Praise:
1.
2.
3.
4.

Prayers:+
1.
2.
3.
4.
Praise:
1.
2.
3.
4.

CHAPTER 6

JUICY TIDBITS TO CONSIDER

WHY DOES EASTER HOP AROUND ON THE CALENDAR EACH YEAR?

Ash Wednesday is always forty-six days before Easter. The first full moon that occurs on or after the spring equinox, which is always March 21st in the Christian Church, determines the date of Easter. This is the first ecclesiastical full moon (known as the 'Paschal' moon) after the spring equinox, which is also why Easter is referred to as 'Pascha.' Therefore, the date that Easter actually falls on annually varies drastically because the dates of the calendar do not consistently correspond to the seasonal cycles of the moon and spring equinox. Check it out for yourself! Note how the date for Easter varies so much from year to year, and this is because of the moon's cycles and when they occur each year after the ecclesiastical spring equinox on March 21st. Remember, however, that no matter what the date of that first full moon is after the equinox—the date that determines Easter each year—simply forty-six days are deducted from it to determine when Ash Wednesday falls. Therefore, the date that Great Lent starts is determined by subtracting forty-six days from the date of Easter, which is determined by the first full moon, which is determined by the solar system, which is determined by God, ad infinitum. Do also note that however much the dates of Easter appear to fluctuate, there are always forty-six days between the start of Great Lent on Ash Wednesday and its conclusion on Easter Sunday.

GREAT LENT ANNUAL DATES: ASH WEDNESDAY— EASTER (PASCHA) SUNDAY EVERY YEAR

03/02/2022–04/17/2022
02/22/2023–04/09/2023
02/14/2024–03/31/2024
03/05/2025–04/20/2025
02/18/2026–04/05/2026
02/10/2027–03/38/2027
03/01/2028–04/16/2028
02/14/2029–04/01/2029
03/06/2030–04/21/2030

SHROVE TUESDAY

The day immediately preceding Ash Wednesday is known as Shrove Tuesday. The word shrove, derived from "shrive," refers to the confession and repentance of sins as a preparation for Lent. But in order to confess or repent of any sins we have to first know what indeed they are. Sometimes it can be the hardest thing for the person themselves to admit that what they are doing is even wrong, or perhaps they honest to God thought it was an okay behavior when in fact it is not. Either way, Shrove Tuesday is an excellent opportunity to dedicate time to reflection of one's thoughts, words, deeds, behaviors, and life over the past months and year. Think about decisions and habits that affect daily life. What is truly taken into the mouth on an hourly basis versus what comes out of it as far as words are concerned? Are these all nourishing for the body or building up for the souls around? Do we rely on someone or something way too much that it often takes the place of the love and trust we should have in our Creator? This can be a valuable time of self-examination, which is so beneficial towards better understanding of oneself that then leads to tremendous spiritual growth. In order to grow though, we have to weed out some old habits and absolutely get rid of them to make new shoots spring up. Take this special Tuesday and consecrate it to the Lord—just between he and you—spending some quiet time in earnest, yet not morbid reflection.

Consider the intimidatingly long (sorry) list of sins and temptations of the world found on pages 19-20. Where have you given in to one, or more, of these temptations and sinned? What pleasures or indulgences could you give up? Or maybe there still is an ever, constant temptation that you need to become aware of so that it does not catch you in a weak moment, causing you to sin. Perhaps you just have a lot of old clutter and "things" that should be gotten rid of, but do not or cannot for whatever reason, and need help to do so. It's part of the Spirit of Lent to confess our sins. Everybody sins because only Jesus is the perfect, innocent Lamb of God who knew no sin. The rest of us continuously fall short of the glory of God. But that is *okay*! It is a constant process of progression and seeking to be closer to God that matters, not that we are perfect all the time. Believe me, Jesus already knows our shortcomings, sins, character defects, problems, and whatever else that holds us back whether we admit it or not. The only disservice we will be doing by not writing it down on paper or confessing it is to ourselves. We are our own worst enemy. And sometimes sin, as it can be the root of our deepest, biggest problems, is a very hard thing to admit or give up, let alone get rid of. It's painful, unpleasant, and by nature bad! But we all have it somewhere in our lives. Kind of similar to the book, *Everybody Poops* . . . we all have, we all do, so don't be in denial or self-righteous about it. So, let's get ready to do some real soul-searching together. Search the last months, weeks, and possibly years in sincere, genuine reflection. Locate those troublesome hurtful areas. Contemplate what you need to do different or what changes could be made to make it better. Know that through all this painstaking labor of unearthing the secrets of past or present, that you are truly seeking God and drawing closer to his grace of ultimate forgiveness and renewing purity. Everlasting hope is at the end of this tunnel so do not fret. Like I always say to my kids, "It is okay to make a mess, just clean it up." Well, confession and admission of sin is the first step in a very valuable process that frees us in Christ. We cannot be forgiven of the sin, or helped with the problem if we do not repent of it. Repentance involves admission of one's fault, or helplessness—or in other words, taking the blame and being accountable. Only then can the grace and peace of Jesus work within us to take that sin away, allowing us to be at peace with God the Father which is the whole reason Christ came. So, let us do our job so that he can do his and everyone will be happy in the end!

FUN LITTLE LIST OF INNOCENT PLEASURES!

A great benefit and blessing that comes from fasting is the renewed ability to take pleasure in the simple joys in life. Because the daily practice revolves around food, and the lack thereof, it has a magical way of simplifying life in general as a result. The more you go without the accustomed pleasure and comfort of food, the more you will have to take refuge in other simple joys and being closer to Christ. Finding continuous inspiration, sustenance, and wisdom in the Word of God is the primary fulfillment of a simple pleasure and comfort that we can replace food with everyday. So, whenever you feel a lack of pleasure or comfort, satisfaction or stimulation, turn to another simple daily pleasure or comfort that aligns with your spiritual walk with the Lord and become filled. This is the point where we say; "Jesus, you are enough," and turn away from other material worldly pleasures. Instead, we turn inward to more godly pleasures of holy living. Most of these are free, and are enhanced by the practice of fasting properly for a long period of time.

On the lines below please fill in your own personal list of simple pleasures, renewed comforts, and joys throughout the entire forty-day long fast. Whenever you encounter a new way to experience joy or an unexpected pleasure, please come back to this page and add it to your growing list, which will hopefully get to be quite long towards the end! You will find that it is necessary to replace the customary pleasure, comfort, and joy that come from food with new and different ones (or more of familiar ones). Again, studying the Word of God is the most important one; but there are many others too that I have discovered and you will too! These can truly be anything that you find you enjoy more and incorporate into your every day. For instance, my list includes some of the following to give examples: hot baths, studying God's Word, taking Pixie (my dog) for walks, listening to music, basking in the warm sun, sewing, burning incense, candles, cooking for my family, spending time with my kids, singing, getting ready for the day, Nordic skiing, reading, watching movies with my husband, etc. It is important to focus on the positive other pleasures, comforts, blessings, and simple joys in your every day lives as you fast because going without food can make one irritable and grumpy. It is paramount to stay focused on all the positives besides food and discover the plethora of pleasure and joy in simple blessings so that we can gain even more heightened awareness as we fast. Keep referring back to this list if in need of inspiration, encouragement, or motivation. Keep adding to it as you discover a new blessing or joy that comes into play and rejoice! It can truly be anything! Another good way to see this is as a list of things we are grateful for. We must count our blessings each day and give thanks to the One who gives them freely! Please, keep this, and add to it always!

"Every good and perfect gift is from above, coming down from the Father of the heavenly lights, who does not change like shifting shadows."

(JAMES 1: 17)

1.
2.
3.
4.
5.
6.
7.
8.
9.
10.
11.
12.
13.
14.
15.
16.
17.
18.
19.
20.
21.
22.
23.
24.
25.
26.

CHAPTER 7

WEEK 1—INTO THE WILDERNESS

VIRTUE OF THE WEEK: GRATITUDE

This week's reading: "It is important for us to distinguish between a desire for food and a hunger for food. It is doubtful whether the average individual reared in our well-fed Western civilization knows much of genuine hunger. The sensation of emptiness or weakness, of gnawing in the pit of the stomach and other symptoms experienced at the outset of a fast are seldom, real hunger. They are a craving for food resulting from the long-continued habit of feeding ourselves three times a day without intermission for 365 days a year.

When the stomach is suddenly denied what it has been in the habit of receiving as its right, it tends to cry out like a spoiled child denied its after-dinner bar of chocolate. Hunger, on the other hand, is a cry from the whole body stemming not from habit but from need. We might say, then, that mere appetite relates to the immediate want of the stomach and true hunger to the real need of the body.

It is strange that any who believe in the biblical revelation should ever have thought that a practice so scriptural as fasting, taught and exemplified by Christ Himself, could ever be harmful to the body, provided it is carried out in accordance with Scripture. The fact is that the very reverse is the case. Fasting makes possible a process of physical therapy. It fully releases the body to operate its own natural system of cleansing and healing.

The loss of appetite, so often the first warning of the approach of acute illness, is thus not only a danger signal but a signpost pointing the way to recovery. It says in effect, "Stop eating, and give your body a chance to recover."

The curative power of fasting has been recognized and applied from ancient times. Plutarch, the famous biographer (ca. AD 46–120) said, "Instead of using medicine, fast a day." Of recent years there has been considerable investigation of this branch of natural therapy by qualified men both in continental Europe and in the United States as well as in Britain, and quite remarkable results have been achieved in clinics in which "the healing fast," as it is sometimes called, is practiced.

Though the spiritual aspects of this subject are of much greater importance, surely the needs of the body—its health and wellbeing—are matters that should concern us too. Our physical condition can often influence our spiritual lives more than we realize. Because the bodies of believers are the temples of the Holy Spirit, as the apostle reminds us, and because they were bought at such a great price, we are to glorify God in them. Is God glorified when our bodies are weak or sickly through neglect of the divine laws that govern their wellbeing? Is God glorified when we become "casualties" in the fight through overworking, overfeeding, or under-nourishing our bodies and failing to give them their "Sabbath" of rest and relaxation?

> In an age of pressure, when the breakdown of mind or body even among professing Christians is becoming all too familiar, the physical value of a fast of God's choosing becomes a matter of some importance. Here is a divine provision for health and healing, for renewal of mind and body, that we must further consider."[1]

SUGGESTED AT-HOME PROJECT:

Write down one of your three temptations and/or sins of the world on a little piece of scrap paper (p. 19-20) and three of your five characteristics of self-will (p. 20-21) on the backside of it. Take the paper privately outside or somewhere where you can burn it and let it go. Give it up to the Lord God —Ashes to ashes, dust to dust.

---

1. Wallis, *God's Chosen Fast*, 110–11.

JOURNEY JOURNAL

Therefore my heart is glad, and my whole being rejoices; my flesh also dwells secure . . . You make known to me the path of life; in your presence there is fullness of joy; at your right hand are pleasures forevermore.

PSALM 16:9, 11

Write at least three goals you have for yourself in this Lenten journey.

DAY 1, ASH WEDNESDAY

Now John wore a garment of camel's hair and a leather belt around his waist, and his food was locusts and wild honey.

MATTHEW 3:4

We begin our journey into the wilderness for forty days of fasting with John the Baptist. He was an ancient holy man who was chosen to reveal the coming of the Messiah. St. John was both humble and powerful at the same time. A true "voice in the wilderness" proclaiming eternal words of life. John the Baptist was so disciplined in how he lived, so righteous, and holy that one must sit back in awe. Well, one of his virtuous ways was fasting. He practiced a form of spiritual fasting where all he lived on was locusts and wild honey. True this is not the *absolute* fasting of no food at all that Jesus, Moses, and other prophets performed; it was a *partial* fast. And that is very interesting because that is what we are doing for forty days—a *partial fast*. Verily, we will have to eat more than locusts and wild honey for the duration, but it is all nonetheless extremely valuable spiritual training to become more pure and more disciplined. "He (John) lived in the desert and practiced a strict life of *askesis* (spiritual training) of which fasting was a major part. St. John is the one who received the revelation that the Messiah had come, that God became incarnate in the person of Jesus. Fasting was essential as he lived out a holy life filled with God's wisdom and strength."[2] I think that from such undeniable evidence of the place value this remarkable practice has, we ought to seek to do it the best we can! It certainly helped make John the Baptist who he was . . . and what a giant bigger than life in character was he. So, strap up those sandals and let's keep marching into the wilderness together, going without food through this entire day until evening when one small, humble meal is allowed. If you can go without it then by all means, do! But you are in line with strict biblical fasting by partaking of one, modest meal after the long, scorching (or freezing) day, so give thanks and be glad for it.

- *10 Minute Meditation*: Sit somewhere, preferably outside, and tune into the sounds around. Get very still and relaxed and clear your mind of all thoughts. Picture yourself out in the wilderness and just be. If and when a thought does come take note of it, and neither dismiss or keep it, but simply acknowledge it and let go.

2. "Fasting: Is It Really Necessary?" lines 16–17.

- *10 Minutes of Prayer:* Select some of your requests, needs, or world problems to pray about and bring them to the Lord.
- *Enter All Data into Personal Daily Record Log.*

JOURNEY JOURNAL

He gives strength to the weary and increases the power of the weak. Even youths grow tired and weary, and young men stumble and fall; but those who hope in the Lord will renew their strength. They will soar on wings like eagles; they will run and not grow weary, they will walk and not be faint.

ISAIAH 40:29–31

Record any initial thoughts, possible fears or hesitations about undertaking this fast in your Journey Journal.

DAY 2, THURSDAY

He must increase; I must decrease.
JOHN 3:30

What did John the Baptist mean when he said these words and how can we apply that to ourselves? I believe he meant that he (John) had to step aside in absolute humility to the Messiah whose "sandals he was unworthy to tie" (John 1:27). Any sense of self-importance, pride, or ego had to be deflated and decreased in light of the one who came to save the world. The more he decreased in importance, being less filled with the self, the more Jesus could increase and dwell inside him spiritually. And this was the ultimate will of God; that Jesus dwells as fully as possible in each of those who believe to give them eternal life. Thus, in order to aspire to the greater will of God, we must decrease our self-will. Fasting is an incredibly effective spiritual tool that helps us humans to decrease the self in all its hindering forms. Reflect back on all those personality characteristics of self-will: self-pitying, self-seeking, selfish, pride, egotistical, and self-importance. These are all various forms of self that we need to work to decrease or get rid of completely because they stand in the way of the LORD God dwelling as fully as possible within us. By denying the bodily self one of its first, and most basic self-wills of satisfying hunger whenever it craves food, we are turning control over to God in trusting dependence. We are not letting the self-will of the body dictate our actions whenever it wants, but we have made a firm, committed decision to go with the higher will of fasting and allow the Holy Spirit to control our action.

The more fasters deny the self-will the more the self decreases and the person is filled with all those personality characteristics of God's-will. As we abstain from eating food and perform other worshipful activities, the Spirit of God increases in all aspects of life. Then the ultimate goal of drawing into closer communion to the LORD God is achieved. Fasting is yet another quiet, peaceful way we can actively seek to communicate with the Lord everyday, wherever we are, in greater communion. As one follower states, "Spirit-power comes from communication with God in prayer and times of quiet meditation. I must constantly seek spirit-communication with God. This is a matter directly between me and God. Those who seek it through the medium of the church do not always get the joy and the wonder of spirit-communication with God. From this communication comes life, joy, peace and healing. Many people do not realize the power that can come to them from direct spirit-communication."[3] As Christians, having the ability to be in constant communication with the Spirit, no matter where we are, is vital to maintaining the joy, love, peace, and worthiness felt at church or other holy places. We have to bring this "spirit-communication" into our daily lives! These are the ways the Lord speaks to us, and placing ourselves in a better place to fully listen and hear those soulful words. And thankfully, being full of gratitude, we can increase the presence of God in our lives through the daily spiritual practices of meditation, fasting, and prayer.

- *Enter All Data for today in the Personal DRL*
- *10 Minutes of Prayer*
- *10 Minutes of Meditation;* "Their strength is to sit still" (Isaiah 30:7). Return to the scripture verse provided most days while meditating if need be to help collect focus, center attention, and direct contemplations towards God. Find strength in knowing that if distracting or intrusive thoughts come you can take refuge in the Word of God by redirecting focus on the scripture verse provided, or coming up with one of your own. Keep and retain these instructions for meditating each day from this day forward.

---

3. Anonymous, *Twenty-Four Hours a Day*, 25–26.

JOURNEY JOURNAL

No discipline seems pleasant at the time, but painful. Later on, however, it produces a harvest of righteousness and peace for those who have been trained by it.

HEBREWS 12:11

Write down what characteristics of self-will you would like to surrender and hand over to be increased and replaced by God's will. (Refer back to the ones you circled or came up with additionally on page 20-21)

DAY 3, FRIDAY—GRATITUDE

Let them give thanks to the Lord for his unfailing love and his wonderful deeds for mankind, for he satisfies the thirsty and fills the hungry with good things.

PSALM 107:8-9

The longer we go without something, the more we are thankful when we can yet have it once again. There is an old saying; "Absence makes the heart grow fond." Well, nothing could be truer when it comes to food as it relates to our heart and stomach! Yes, we love it. Yes, we miss it so incredibly much the longer we go without it, however, we are also full of incomparable, unfailing gratitude all the more for it in the absence. For those of you who have had to go without a spouse for a number of weeks, or perhaps been separated from a dear friend or family member for a duration of time, you know how much your heart longs for them, how it aches in the space between. And then how full the heart becomes with pure gratitude and joy when reunited with the loved one at long last. Well, many blessings operate in quite the same way: loved ones, food, shelter, friends, clothes, health, the weather, etc. The list of blessings could go on ad infinitum because the good Lord has given us so incredibly much to be grateful for. "You will be enriched in every way so that you can be generous on every occasion, and through us your generosity will result in thanksgiving to God" (2 Corinthians 9:11). But what about the most common blessings of food, our house, our children, our spouse, our health, our God, our very life, that can be all too easy to take for granted because we have them everyday? Yet these are the greatest and most important blessings in life and truly all we have. To become truly grateful, content, and overflowing with thanksgiving to the Giver of all these perfect treasures on earth is a daily task. You may ask; "Well, how do I become more grateful for these great yet most simple blessings on a daily basis?" The answer is simple: go without them for a while and see how much you truly miss them, start to think about them in different ways, how suddenly important they become to you, and how much gratitude you overflow with when reunited with them again. For instance, we take a shower almost every day . . . But go camping for a week out in the dirty wilderness and see how much every square inch of you longs for a shower, yearns for that renewed cleanliness that we take for granted on a daily basis. Then, feel the raw, pure, naked gratitude as the water washes over your caked, dirty body when at long last you finally get to take a shower again. Food works exactly the same way. Go without it for a day or two; or simply all day like you are hopefully doing right now, and see how often you think about it, how much your stomach yearns for it, and how much more grateful you are for its reality when you sit down for that one simple meal at night. Now, after going hungry for a while, you are brought to the enlightened state of true, pure emotion and state of gratitude when you can finally sit down and eat once again. Thanksgiving overflows from the heart upwards towards our heavenly Father as we give earnest, deeply more meaningful thanks for this food in front of us than we might on a regular, everyday basis. Fasting helps us be truly grateful for the incredible blessings that we have in a new way as never before. It helps us learn to be content with these simple, common, and yet greatest of all blessings in complete thankfulness and praise. No longer do we, as the body of Christ, fall into the temptation of taking these most important blessings of life for granted. On the contrary, we fast from them; purposefully taking them away so that we can be fully enlightened to their eternal place in our lives and feel pure gratitude towards God for creating them in such beauteous splendor and bestowing them upon us.

- *Meditate for 10 minutes*, focusing on being filled with the heightened state of emotional Gratitude that comes from fasting. Lift your heart upwards in quiet, worshipful praise of God who gives us all good things.
- *Pray for 10 minutes*, reviewing your list of prayer requests and problems from earlier.
- *Enter All Data in Personal DRL.*

JOURNEY JOURNAL

Write down at least five simple, common blessings of Life that you are grateful for in the Journey Journal. Food for thought: If fasting is a way to increase our gratitude for food what are some possible spiritual ways you could increase gratitude for other common blessings?

DAY 4, SATURDAY

Putting the Creator in Creativity

Explanation of Creative Space Page:

The Creative Space Page each Saturday is an *optional activity* and is exactly that: an opportunity for you to unleash and exercise your unique creativity in whatever way you wish—on or off the page! Of course, you can fill the page itself with anything creative, using artsy pens, paint, or crayons or whatever medium suits your whims of fancy . . . Or you can do a creative project or truly anything that takes creativity off the page! Perhaps draw a picture of what you did on the page, or maybe just write about it on the blank page itself (or not and leave it blank). For instance, you could sew something, or bake cookies, or do a kids craft project, or decorate the house, or garden, or whatever!

For men this may include anything with tools—a house project, painting, fixing the car, yard work, playing a game with the kids or grandkids, handyman work, or whatever appeals to your creative imagination. It might even include reading something highly creative such as fantasy or poetry or science fiction. Whatever relaxes you into your creative space totally qualifies. Indulge in a hobby that you haven't had the chance to for a while or teach the dog a new trick! It is a subscribed time for each of us to tap into those immense, although often neglected, powers that bring us closer to our Creator. Whatever you end up doing, try to make some record of it to share with the group, or a friend, if you are doing the study on your own. Make a point to share! And if you choose not to do the Creative Space page this week, or another week, that is okay too. Please, keep in mind this is a strict fasting day so the same rules apply as other weekdays in regards to food.

As you engage in your creative endeavor think about the qualities that you are actively showing—such as gentleness, self-control, love, precision, attention to detail, beauty, magnifying creation—that God has given you. Contemplate how we magnify His Creation in what we ourselves do and are channels of his grace. Let it flow through you in whatever you do and let it bring you into closer communion with the Original, One Source of all things. For instance, I personally love to make clothes. My mother is an incredible seamstress and so was her mother, my grandma. The same talent for sewing and making beautiful clothes must run in my blood too because when I sit down behind a sewing machine it is like making music to my fingers. Where some might become bored with the intricacies of sewing, I love to explore the world of fabrics, endless details, and seams! But each to their own ... So indulge in whatever creative fantasy may come. May peace, love, joy, and happiness accompany you in the process!

Creative Space Page

Record *any* and *everything* you eat and at what exact time in the DRL. This is never an option. It is always mandatory and one of the 3 cardinal rules.

QUADRAGESIMA SUNDAY
"FORTIETH" FREE DAY

Further Explanation of Sundays during Lent:

As mentioned in the 'About the Study' section in the beginning of this study, Sundays are *free* days on which we do not fast. However, one should still limit the amount of wine to one glass or one beer and not indulge too much in food, or overeat. Your body is in fasting mode and to go hog wild and just eat like crazy is not in line with the spirit. It would be very counterproductive and just make it harder for you the rest of the time. Sure, relax and eat at random times, whenever you want really, but still listen to your body and do not eat past satiation. Eat small amounts and graze on tastes you may have missed, but do not engorge. Do not stuff yourself or overeat because this will just work against you come Monday morning, I promise! Enjoy good foods with moderation and carry what you have learned so far into the choices you make on these important Sundays. Use it as a personal time to blend the new fasting lifestyle with your old, normal one into a beautiful new creation that honors and glorifies God. Remember and retain some of the changes and ways you have had to adjust during the week, while loosening up and allowing the Lord to work in your life in new, awesome ways. None of the fasting rules apply on Sundays, (except to keep your alcohol consumption to extreme moderation), and not stuff the stomach too full, since this could be detrimental to the overall progressive spiritual journey of the body and soul. Also, do try to keep all the healthy, good habits encouraged in the fasting rules on these days as it will be easier on your body and better for establishing the replacement of old bad habits to new better ones. Try not to just overdo it on sweets, meat, dairy, or anything that is not typically allowed.

My soul will be satisfied as with fat and rich food, when I remember you upon my bed, and *meditate* on you in the watches of the night.

PSALM 63:5-6

DAY 5, MONDAY

Then Jesus was led by the Spirit into the wilderness to be tempted by the devil. And after fasting forty days and forty nights, he was hungry.
MATT 4:1

Who is this Spirit that leads Jesus into the wilderness where he spent forty days and forty nights fasting? "God is Spirit, and those who worship him must worship in spirit and truth" (John 4: 24). Jesus follows the Spirit of God into the wilderness, and we follow Jesus and the Spirit, also into the wilderness of temptation to fast for forty days and forty nights. The Spirit is an extremely important reality to grasp in the whole idea and execution of fasting because it is done as a *spiritual* practice. Like the *askesis* mentioned earlier as a form of spiritual training done by John the Baptist, fasting is a discipline that must be practiced in order to be effective. Similar to going on a run, our bodies build up a stamina, or natural endurance to it. The first time you go for a run you can't go very far, just like the first day of fasting is the hardest. Then, the next day you run a little further, then the next are able to run a little further, as your body builds up endurance to running; your body will also build up natural endurance to fasting for longer and longer periods of time. In other words, similar to running, fasting is an actual activity—something our bodies physically do—from which the benefits can only become fully known through raw, faithful action. One cannot simply read about it in order to receive the very real spiritual benefits fasting has to offer. Sometimes these quieter spiritual practices—such as prayer, meditation, and fasting—are misunderstood for not being great in action, but they are in fact some of the most powerful. They require great restraint, focus, and concentrated effort to be done well. Sometimes it is much, much harder to sit and do "nothing" (which is not what meditation actually is anyways) than it is to run a dozen errands. On the same note, it is much harder to exercise self-control and mindfulness in regard to food by not eating anything all day long, than it is to just eat to be eating whenever the impulse arises. Praying, for instance, may also seem as though it were not a great action, but it is one of the greatest actions we can do each day. "Better is a handful of quietness than two hands full of toil and a striving after wind" (Ecclesiastes 4: 6).

It is also this spirit of restraint and self-control that can be applied directly to the sins and temptations we encounter in life. By simply being quiet, gentle, and refraining from doing them anymore (if they have already become a vicious cycle, an everyday habit) then we are performing a great feat indeed. Let us *fast* from temptation and sin itself, and see that every time we resist the impulsive desire to eat, we also see past the food itself and resist whatever other bad habits or dreadful sins may be there. In this way, we are daily working on giving up, and not giving in, to the temptations of first food, second self-will, third . . . Work your way down the list recorded earlier and contemplate what those habitual sins, temptations, or personality defects are that could better be done without. Then, whenever you consciously bypass the temptation to eat and are fasting from food, also consciously draw into your awareness the presence of what else you could do without and *fast* from those thoughts, words, or deeds as much as possible. I know it is difficult, but just like running, the more you do it, the easier it becomes. And the reward is so huge! To become more and more like Jesus as we follow Him into the wilderness is to become stronger and more resilient against sin itself just as he was. Going without food helps build our spirit's endurance, resolve, faith, discipline, and purity against the evil one. So, bite your lip and know that in restraining from each tempting bite of food, you are hopefully also learning to resist those pressing and real temptations and sins of the world. You are building up your armor in Christ to face anything in the world that might attempt to dissuade or disillusion.

- *Meditate for 10 minutes*; focusing on being filled with the Spirit. Know that you are already everything you need to be and become aware of your own states of emotional/spiritual being starting always in Peace.
- *Pray for 10 minutes*, knowing that it is a great action with provable, tangible results that could not be attained by all our busy "actions."
- *Enter All Data in Personal DRL*

JOURNEY JOURNAL

Write down any thoughts, feelings, or concerns that you may want to express to the Lord today in the journey journal.

DAY 6, TUESDAY

For the law of the Spirit of life has set you free in Christ Jesus from the law of sin and death . . . For those who live according to the flesh set their minds on the things of the flesh, but those who live according to the Spirit set their minds on the things of the Spirit. For to set the mind on the flesh is death, but to set the mind on the Spirit is life and peace.

ROMANS 8:2, 5-6

The desires of the flesh are many and if consumed in excess—or some at all, even once—very sinful. The flesh lusts after other flesh, after food, material objects, wealth, endless pleasures, alcohol, sex, without considering why. All of these desires, or temptations, lead us eventually into sin if we cannot maintain self-control. These deeds of the flesh lead us farther away from God, spiraling down a shallow bankrupt path that ends in spiritual death. This is why we completely deny the flesh when we fast for the Lord. We put on the armor of salvation and follow in his footsteps as true, faithful soldiers of the Word. "Whoever says he abides in him ought to walk in the same way in which he walked" (1 John 2: 6). Well, Jesus fasted for forty days and forty nights, and so are we! Not to compare ourselves as even coming close to any sort of the perfection exhibited by Christ; yet by denying food to the body whenever it gets hungry, fasting teaches us to likewise deny the flesh and overcome its constant impulses. It sanctifies us, in a way, and strengthens the Spirit to overcome the mortal flesh in all our cries for more food, addictions of every sort, and constant pleasures. Like a little toddler that cries for a toy or immediate gratification, so does our flesh cry out like babies for more material satisfactions. It lusts after jewelry, tasty things, parading about, in all manners of greed. And when it does not receive its instant gratification to "feel better," no matter how short the fix may be, we rebel. However, in fasting we discipline our flesh by denying it every impulse for food and submitting the self-will to God's will. This submission to the Holy Spirit allows it to dwell in us as fully as possible, giving the Lord ample room to work through us for his good pleasure. In this way, we are controlled by the Holy Spirit and not by the selfish desires of self. The ego and self-centered nature gradually deflates itself the more it is denied sovereign power and submits to Thee sovereign power. Instead the self becomes more selfless, alive in the Spirit of Christ, full of those precious gifts of gratitude, love, self-control, truth, and humility. All one has to do is surrender to the magic of life in the Spirit, finding newness each day in the wonder of those "who walk not according to the flesh but according to the Spirit" (Romans 8: 4).

- *Meditate for 10 minutes*; filling your entire being with the Spirit of Christ. Breathe out the self with its material desires. Breathe in clarity and purity. Breathe out stress and unnecessary thoughts. Breathe in joy and peace. Relax.
- *Pray for 10 minutes.*
- *Enter All Data in Personal DRL.*

JOURNEY JOURNAL

Write down what earthly pleasures and desires of the flesh you could do without. How might resisting the urge to eat when hungry help this?

Therefore be imitators of God, as beloved children.
Ephesians 5:1

Let us not become weary in doing good, for at the proper time we will reap a harvest if we do not give up.
Galatians 6:9

DAY 7, WEDNESDAY

So then, brothers, we are debtors, not to the flesh, to live according to the flesh. For if you live according to the flesh you will die, but if by the Spirit you put to death the deeds of the body, you will live. For you did not receive the spirit of slavery to fall back into fear, but you have received the Spirit of adoption as sons, by whom we cry, "Abba! Father!" . . . provided we suffer with him in order that we may also be glorified with him.

ROMANS 8:12–15, 17

Elevated by the separation fasting creates from the material, (the flesh), into the spiritual is partaking in the new life. We free ourselves from our old, sinful, fleshy self and take on newfound serenity, joy, and knowledge in the Spirit. True contentment comes at last; not just the immediate, soulless quenching of food for the stomach—but an everlasting home full of beauty beyond material worth. No food passed Jesus' lips for forty days! Now let every time we consciously deny to give in to the cravings of the flesh and take of food—or maybe another addiction—that we are imitating Christ in His purity, in His strength, in His battle against the Devil. Let us remember that we are doing this to become purer—to become more perfect—as He was in complete, utter perfection, the Lamb of God. Fasting helps us become more like Christ because he set us an example for doing it first himself in order to overcome sin. Thus, He sanctioned fasting to be a powerful, spiritual tool used in part for the purpose of conquering sin here on earth. Therefore, we ought to confess our sins, be truly repentant for them, while lastly giving them over to Jesus to ultimately forgive and remove completely. This is the goal of every Lenten season and fasting truly does help focus on this most valuable process, intrinsic to the Christian faith. After fasting for a long, long time without eating anything, Jesus must have been starving. The longest I have personally every gone without food is five nights and six days and I thought I was going to faint! Yet somehow in all this suffering for the sake of renewal, for rebirth, for becoming more Christ-like, there is the ultimate hope of being truly forgiven all our sins, completely purified, and thus in a greater state of perfection, and closer to the King of Heaven. Evaluate and access each moment-to-moment decision of what we take into our bodies . . . eating nothing is better than a whole lot of unhealthy nonsense. It is so much more beneficial to consume absolutely nothing except water or healthy drinks all day, than to eat highly processed foods laden with chemicals, or too much food. Just say no and keep the gates (the lips) of the body closed rather than loosely letting past all kinds of dirty traffic into the pure vessel of the body. True, we will never be able to come even close to the perfection of Christ, however, it is the everyday commitment in attempting to do so that matters to him. Such personal sacrifice shows our faith and dedication to following in his paths of righteousness and makes us worthier to declare his name. Along the journey, although extremely hard, we inevitable come to know our Savior unfathomably better, drawing closer into His unshakeable bonds of love, holding us forever near.

- *Meditate for 10 minutes*: becoming as still as a statue. Envision yourself as part of the unmovable, permanent objects of the earth: rocks, trees, buildings, etc. Sink into a deep sense of peace as "you also, like living stones, are being built into a spiritual house to be a holy priesthood, offering spiritual sacrifices acceptable to God through Jesus Christ" (1 Peter 2: 5).
- *Pray for 10 minutes.*
- *Enter All Data in Personal DRL.*

JOURNEY JOURNAL

I can do all this through him who gives me strength.
PHILIPPIANS 4:13

Write down a few questions you would ask Jesus in the wilderness of fasting in your Journey Journal, along with any other thoughts, feelings or concerns you may be experiencing today.

CHAPTER 8

WEEK 2—MIND OVER MATTER; SPIRIT OVER FLESH

VIRTUE OF THE WEEK: PATIENCE

This week's reading:

"In the orthodox world, we use the word "passions" to describe tendencies that each person has that lead us to sin. Each of us has a "passion" for anger, lust, power, greed, ego, etc. We do not get through life without wrestling with each of these sometimes on a daily basis. The most basic "passion" is hunger. While we can go a day without a lustful thought or an angry thought, we can't go more than a few hours without a hungry thought. So, if we can tame our passion for eating, we can hopefully tame our other passions. If we can discipline ourselves to go without certain kinds of food, we can hopefully discipline ourselves so that we can go without certain kinds of behavior that are spiritually destructive. Thus, fasting is not about giving up something only to get it back. Fasting is about getting control of our passions, maintaining control over them, and ultimately giving control of ourselves to God."[1]

---

1. Akrotirianakis, "And When You Fast," lines 6–14.

SUGGESTED AT-HOME ACTIVITY FOR THIS WEEK:

Get a hammer and 2 nails. Take them outside and find a tree somewhere convenient. Write down your three temptations or sins of the world on a piece of paper as well as your five personality characteristics of self-will. Nail it to the tree and leave it there for one week . . . until next Wednesday . . . (somewhere nobody will see it!)

You also must be patient. Keep your hopes high, for the day of the Lord's coming is near.

JAMES 5:8

Hot tempers cause arguments, but patience brings peace.

PROVERBS 15:18

The end of something is better than its beginning. Patience is better than pride.

ECCLESIASTES 7:8

DAY 8, THURSDAY

"Yet even now," declares the Lord, "return to me with all your heart, with fasting, with weeping, and with mourning; and rend your hearts and not your garments." Return to the LORD your God, for he is gracious and merciful, slow to anger, and abounding in steadfast love.

JOEL 2:12-13

No matter how bad it gets or what suffering there is; no matter how big the problem is; how hopeless, how miserable, there is always a solution! Jesus. None of us get through life without having our fair share of trials. Sometimes these trials are caused by ourselves; we make mistakes, make the wrong choices, we fail. It is a part of human existence "for all have sinned and fall short of the glory of God" (Romans 3: 23). But do not despair! It is in those hardest of times that Jesus is there the most. When we are completely broken, that is when he is most ready to pick us up and save. When we are miserable, lonely, and depressed; that is when he most wants to provide comfort and reprieve. He is the greatest Healer of all time and there is no spiritual ill or malady that he cannot cure with faith. It does not matter how low we may have sunk, or the terrible thing we may have done that caused it. What matters to him is that we come to him for the solution, for the grace to be saved from all our troubles. There are many ways we *return* into his loving arms of comfort; and one of those is with *fasting*. He asks us to fast from the heart, as a sign of the humble acknowledgement of our human state—in need of his everlasting grace. The burdens of life are too much and they cause much weeping, much mourning, over the sadness and pain that inevitably comes at some point. The problems of the world are too heavy to carry alone and may break us if we do not give them over to the LORD. He is the only One who can truly help to solve them. We simply cannot do it on our own. And in many cases, neither can doctors, psychiatrists, or any other person on earth. So much sadness, so much heartache, so much everything gone awry in this crazy, chaotic world we live in today that the only solution is to return to the One who can truly heal. Give it over to him with tears, and with fasting, and he will take his sheep into those loving arms once more.

I find it interesting that Jesus speaks of the *heart* twice in the same sentence. It makes it seem that these problems that cause us to weep and mourn are matters of the heart. That maybe only he can truly know what is the cause of our deepest sorrows. Maybe things become so complicated and convoluted that we are past the point of being able to explain or rationalize it to anyone and just weep. Or perhaps we have lost someone nearer and dearer to our heart than life itself, and nobody else really knows or understands except him. See, he knows everything about what we are going through already, and why it is so painful. He knows the depth of our suffering and why, and speaks to our heart because he loves us and has called us by name. Out of the amazing qualities of his love for us, he implores us (almost begs) us to come back to him—to stay by his side once again. In this return, one must *rend* their hearts. This means they must wring out their heart of any hidden deeds, impure thoughts, or vileness. Therefore, in order to completely make a successful return into the loving arms of Jesus, the heart must be purified so that he can make the soul clean. We must be honest about what is in each of our own hearts before the LORD, so that he can truly take away these burdens and forgive us our sins. Fasting is a great spiritual weapon that helps us do just this. Fasting helps us examine our hearts and purify ourselves in this epic journey of faith. It enhances our personal walk of faith with the Shepherd, and gives us the necessary tools to immediately return to him if we go astray. Fasting, like meditation and prayer, helps give us the power to commune with the Holy Spirit, whenever and wherever we are. It is especially effective at bringing us back to the LORD if we become lost in the wilderness of temptation and sin. It is a personal relationship of grace and faith with the Savior and all we must do to receive the guaranteed gift of healing and grace, is be honest with him in our heart of hearts and desire to *rend* our heart of anything that keeps us from returning to his arms of eternal love.

- *Meditate for 10 minutes.* "Be still, and know that I am God" (Psalm 46: 10). Remember to come back to the Scripture verse for a return of focus and clarity.
- *Pray for 10 minutes.*
- *Enter All Data in Personal DRL.*

JOURNEY JOURNAL

Write down anything you may be suffering from in the Journey Journal. Are there things that are making you weep or mourn? Please, write about them to the LORD. Also, write down possible causes of these—known or unknown.

Come to me, all you who are weary and burdened, and I will give you rest.

MATTHEW 11:28

DAY 9, FRIDAY—PATIENCE

But if we hope for what we do not yet have, we wait for it patiently.

ROMANS 8:25

When only one small meal in the evening is allowed each night of this long fast, the virtue of patience is cultivated as the believer learns to wait patiently for that meal at the end of the day. All day long no food should pass through the lips, although a 20-ounce nutrient drink may be drunk such as V8 or Odwalla green machine, for sustenance. In this waiting all the livelong day for that single, wonderful hot meal around sundown, patience builds up in the soul and fortifies the spirit. No longer is it allowed to give in to every impulse or impatient desire, but we must learn to be patient and control the flesh, and the stomach until the reward comes. This fasting process which cultivates and installs much patience in the one who does it, is quite opposite of how modern day society tells us we should live. Modernism tells us to satisfy our flesh with instant gratification constantly. There is no such thing as waiting for what you *really* want anymore. Everyone is in such a rush they will practically run you over with impatience for the slightest bit of having to wait. Take Amazon for instance, or Facebook: whatever in the whole wide universe you want, just click your little finger and it will appear within a few short days—maybe even one day! You do not have to wait to get what you want to obtain your reward in this modern day society. On the contrary, you can have whatever you wish right away, as soon as you want it, with absolutely no delay necessary. Need more friends? Just log in and click your fingers again on a screen to have hundreds of instant likes or more superficial friends. Need a bride? Mail order one from China or the Philippines! Nobody needs to cultivate or show patience in anything anymore and that is exactly why so many people are so very impatient and have no time for anyone or anything else but themselves. This society breeds selfishness, impatience and greed. That is why fasting is so counterculture, so exotic, so undeniably virtuous. That is also why you should be careful about telling just anybody in these modern times about it because I can almost guarantee you they will not understand. This is an ancient spiritual discipline, most commonly practiced thousands of years ago . . . not today. And it does require much, much patience on behalf of the faster in order to do correctly. So, just know and enjoy the assurance that with each long hour that passes you are obtaining more patience in your store of spiritual treasures! The longer you learn to wait to eat food the better your spiritual bank of patience! Perhaps you may find that you are then able to draw from this larger, increased store of precious ability at other crucial times in your life. When everyone else is racing by 100 mph, you can have the advantage of some extra patience due to the meals you have not consumed yet today to gain the upper hand. Even with the kids . . . I have three boys that constantly test this virtue, which you think I should have plenty in store of by now, but . . . It still is a struggle sometimes! In waiting, we rely on God and demonstrate our complete dependence and faith in him. We actively practice and cultivate this virtue through all the waiting for forty long days as we fast for him alone.

- *Meditate for 10 minutes*; "He went out to the field one evening to meditate, and as he looked up, he saw camels approaching" (Genesis 24: 63).
- *Pray for 10 minutes.*
- *Enter All Data in Personal DRL.*

JOURNEY JOURNAL

So as to walk in a manner worthy of the Lord, fully pleasing to him: bearing fruit in every good work and increasing in the knowledge of God; being strengthened with all power, according to his glorious might, for all endurance and patience with joy.

COLOSSIANS 1: 10-11

Write down 3-5 other "rewards" besides food that you may have to wait patiently for. (Ex. A trip somewhere, a new bike rack, Christmas, summer fun, certain house projects made possible, etc.) How are all these "rewards" similar and yet different from our having to wait patiently to eat food while fasting?

DAY 10, SATURDAY

Creative Space Page

Record *any* and *everything* you eat and exactly at what time in the DRL. This is never an option. It is always mandatory and one of the three cardinal rules.

REMINISCERE SUNDAY

"Remember"

Free Day

Quick Friendly Reminder: Please, please, please, do not overeat or drink too much today. I say this as a warning in your best interest; it will only be harder for you to fast tomorrow and the rest of the days. It is sort of like starting over if you eat too much, or too much of the wrong thing . . . Your body is already adjusting to the strict limitations of fasting and cleansing itself of all the impurities. And like most things, it is harder in the beginning. So many things are harder at the very start, but once you are underway actually get easier. For example, a conversation, a work out, a relationship, an essay, a long journey, is always harder at the start. Well, fasting is the same way! So, don't set yourself back in the process by overdoing it with too much (if any) of what's not in the strict fasting rule, or it will just keep making it harder come tomorrow!

Take this opportunity to do any manner of free writing in the Journey Journal below as an option every Sunday, if desirable. New foods tried, better drink substitutes, or ideas that you would like to do differently this next week can be written here, along with any questions, concerns, or ideas that you may have—or may even want to share.

JOURNEY JOURNAL

DAY 11, MONDAY

Do not be led away by diverse and strange teachings, for it is good for the heart to be strengthened by grace, not by foods, which have not benefited those devoted to them.

HEBREWS 13:9

Well, the Bible is very clear here that to be *devoted* to foods is not at all beneficial for the person. Rather, it is *good for the heart* to be continually strengthened by God's grace. So important is this focus on the heavenly things of the Holy Spirit such as grace, mercy, and humility instead of the material focus of such earthly things as food, houses, cars, and all the things money can buy. If we choose to put our devotion and commitment into such transient blessings as food (or material things) we could miss the eternal richness of blessings that God wants to give us for putting our complete devotion and commitment in him! All the beautiful riches of the Spirit are ours so long as we dwell as completely and closely as possible with the Lord, far above letting temporal distractions hinder this progress. "Therefore, since we are surrounded by so great a cloud of witnesses, let us also lay aside every weight, and sin which clings so closely, and let us run with endurance the race that is before us, looking to Jesus, the founder and perfecter of our faith, who for the joy that was set before him endured the cross, despising the shame, and is seated at the right hand of the throne of God" (Hebrews 12: 1–2). It takes commitment; it takes *devotion* to run a race with endurance. So does forty days of fasting. And just like running an endurance race, fasting strengthens our heart by producing great spiritual growth. It makes us stronger, more temperate, faithful people of God who observe this ancient discipline that has been so neglected in the modern day church.

Of course, food is good for you! I'm not saying that it is not. But being *devoted* to it is not beneficial or healthy. Being too *devoted* to a variety of other material, earthly things such as our possessions, our spouse, or even our own children, is not necessarily beneficially either. We ought to have a healthy relationship to these earthly blessings that God has put us over as stewards, but not be enslaved or overly consumed by them. That would almost imply an idolatrous relationship with these very amazing material blessings that have been so entrusted. But we ought not love these earthly things too much; certainly not more than we love Jesus Christ, or else we will get into spiritual danger. "Whoever loves father or mother more than me is not worthy of me. And whoever loves son or daughter more than me is not worthy of me" (Matt 10: 37). As you can see I have substituted the reality of love with that of devotion for they are very close in reality. We are devoted to what and whom we love, just as we love what we are most devoted to. This is a truth of the heart and whom it chooses to be devoted to and why. God's grace is good for the heart and strengthens the believer, whereas food (and setting one's mind too much on other earthly blessings) is not beneficial. Fasting helps us accomplish this healthy balance in the relationship to material earthly things with a spiritual mindset of Christ. It helps us find the correct proportions of love and devotion to give to our priorities while keeping the lion's share for the Ruler of all.

- *Meditate for 10 minutes.* Select a favorite scripture to have in the back of your mind during meditation and if or when you have a distracting thought, capture it by the Holy Spirit, and let thought itself return to that one scripture verse. And then once thought is gone, let the spirit fully occupy once again. Repeat this process of returning the mindful thought back to your scripture verse every time you have an intrusive thought until your thought-plane becomes elevated in purity.
- *Pray for 10 minutes.*
- *Enter All Data in Personal DRL.*

JOURNEY JOURNAL

Do not lay up for yourselves treasures on earth, where moth and rust destroy and where thieves break in and steal, but lay up for yourselves treasures in heaven, where neither moth nor rust destroys and where thieves do not break in and steal. For where your treasure is, there your heart will be also.

MATTHEW 6: 19-21

How can becoming too overly devoted to something be unhealthy for our spirit? What are a few things besides food that you may be too devoted to? Write down some ways that you may be able to distance yourself in a healthy way from these—with the help of Christ, and possibly using some of the spiritual techniques from fasting to gain insight.

DAY 12, TUESDAY

"God is committed to rewarding those acts of the human heart that signify human helplessness and hope in God. Over and over again in Scripture God promises to come to the aid of those who stop depending on themselves and seek God as their treasure and help."[2]
—JOHN PIPER

One of my absolute favorite books that had incredible influence on me when I first came to the practice of fasting is *A Hunger for God*, by John Piper. I learned so much from this great scholar with a beautiful heart and soul along the journey into this mysterious, sometimes scary world. His words quoted above and again below speak to the heart and reverberate truth across time and space into the soul. How is fasting an act of the human heart that signifies helplessness and expresses a hope in God? In many ways it brings the believer into a vulnerable state where we forsake our personal, human needs and comforts, and give them over to Jesus our Redeemer. To allow ourselves to go hungry for the sake of our faith is reducing ourselves into a condition of humility where we are forced to rely more on God. Without food there is little else to keep us from feeling helpless. From that helplessness and lack of dependence on the self (because all the self is in unpleasant hunger) the spirit must arise and aspire to the heavenly realms in hope of preservation. Going hungry really does cause one to feel helpless and quite vulnerable sometimes, and the only choice possible to take away those scary feelings is to place them into our Creator. We must put all our faith into something greater because we are so thoroughly weakened. Therefore, the faster must transfer all his or her typical feelings of self-reliance, solidarity, dependence, and trust from the self over to God.

A newfound hope blooms as the relationship between God and us humans through Jesus Christ grows exponentially as we feel ourselves drawn irreversibly closer into his presence. Many rewards, spiritual experiences, and untold gifts result as we give over our very selves over to his almighty will. We truly become like a little child depending solely on Our Father for every love and human need. He becomes the Source, most immediate, most powerful, at the center of our life—as essential for our continued existence as the source of food is. It is also an act of the human heart because we are sacrificing something very near and dear to our heart . . . food! Of course, we love it! All those delicious medleys and parade of flavors to live for . . .

2. Piper, *Hunger for God*, 159.

but in giving them up for the sake of Jesus we are showing that we love Him more than satisfying our human longing and need for food! That is an act of our very heart of hearts when we forsake things we like, our personal attachments and comforts out of love for him. "The final answer is that God rewards fasting because fasting expresses the cry of the heart that nothing on the earth can satisfy our souls besides God. God must reward this cry because God is most glorified in us when we are most satisfied in him."[3] We are actively saying with the action of fasting that God is better than any delicious satisfaction that can be found in food and we actively, always *want* him more. Fasting tests the desires of the human heart, what truly motivates a person, and where they put their hope and faith. All of these parts of the higher self should be invested in God, and not continuously in the pleasures and satisfactions of the flesh. Fasting teaches us how to do that in a way that is pleasing and acceptable to God.

- *Meditate for 10 minutes.* "Keep this Book of the Law always on your lips; meditate on it day and night, so that you may be careful to do everything written in it. Then you will be prosperous and successful" (Joshua 1: 8).
- *Pray for 10 minutes.*
- *Enter All Data in Personal DRL.*

---

3. Piper, *Hunger for God*, 162.

JOURNEY JOURNAL

Write down anything you want to relay to your Creator. Any thoughts, feelings, concerns in the whole wide world!

DAY 13, WEDNESDAY—DISCIPLINE

It is for discipline that you have to endure. God is treating you as sons. For what son is there whom his father does not discipline? . . . For the moment all discipline seems painful rather than pleasant, but later it yields the peaceful fruit of righteousness to those who have been trained by it.

HEBREWS 12:7, 11

There are many things in life that we want to achieve but some days on the road to that great prize do not want to put in the work to get there. Take college for instance. Sure, a degree would be fantastic, sure the friends and parties are great, but aren't there so many days and nights that you just don't feel like studying? It takes discipline to sit there for hours on end and study books so that you can pass the exams to move on in the world. There are many times we are not in the "mood" to do something or really do not even want to, and would much rather be doing something else. But we do it anyways because we are working towards a far greater reward than momentary desires or temporal satisfactions. It takes discipline to keep our decisions focused on what needs to take place, and do what we are supposed to do in order to advance. This is also called living life with a *purpose* and not just any ole way you want, when you want. There are many, many other achievements in life that take tremendous discipline as well in order to succeed. Take work, a huge one, for example. It's not like you can just say to your boss, "O, I would rather not be here right now; I'm not having any fun today, so I am going to go home." No, one has to be disciplined with their work and career so that they can get done what they need in order to accomplish certain goals along the way. Sure, there are many days you would rather be doing something else, or certain tasks and jobs that are odious; but you have to do them anyways because that is the job. It takes discipline to do those tasks you really do not like, but must do, because they are part of the work that constitutes the total job. Sure they are unpleasant (and sometimes just plain painful) at the time, but you endure through it so that you can perform the job correctly and get the reward.

    Fasting actually has this virtue as part of the very nature of its definition as it is continually denoted an ancient spiritual *discipline*. And similar to many other essential components of life; fasting teaches us and installs in the faster this weighty quality. The old, worn out saying, 'the best things in life do not happen overnight," is reminiscent of the amount of endurance, discipline and patience it takes to achieve them. Doing well at work, school, sports, and even lasting relationships takes all these virtues to truly succeed. The golden reward does not come overnight, nor does just anyone receive it. One must prove one's ability to persevere through the hard times, the very unpleasant times, on the already difficult road towards victory. Those times may even be *painful*. Does a baby just come out overnight with all its immortal joy and splendor for the world to behold? No! It takes great pain and sacrifice on behalf of the mother to grow and give birth. Take sports for example: can the Nordic skier say to himself before the race, "O, it is too cold out today to train, or it is snowing too much today to go?" No! They go out anyways, in brutally tough conditions and train to keep up their life goals of winning the race! The help of discipline enters a person's very character and bestows itself deep down in their very soul. Then during those tough times of difficulty, or on those bad days when we just do not feel like doing it anymore, that immense store of discipline that we have been diligently building up, comes to our aid and keeps us on track like a glorious north star shining bright. It helps keep us focused on the correct priorities and the bigger goals we are working towards and not just the momentary fleeting issues with self-will or emotions. In the same way, fasting is by nature a difficult road to walk with the Lord, but just like he promises us in Scripture there is much spiritual fruit such as peace, ability to endure, and righteousness if we persevere through the tough moments (in this case hunger). Discipline is considered so great a quality to have in the Bible that it is an end unto itself—it is the goal and reason we endure. "It is for discipline that you have to endure" (Hebrews 12: 7). And, we should be grateful while we endure since God has chosen us to receive this experience.

- *Meditate for 10 minutes.*
- *Pray for 10 minutes.* "But when you pray, go into your room, close the door and pray to your Father, who is unseen. Then your Father, who sees what is done in secret, will reward you" (Matthew 6: 6).
- *Enter All Data in Personal DRL.*

JOURNEY JOURNAL

My son, do not regard lightly the discipline of the Lord, nor be weary when reproved by him. For the Lord disciplines the one he loves, and chastises every son whom he receives.

HEBREWS 12:5-6

Write down one other component of your life that takes discipline besides fasting. How does discipline help you get through the tough times and endure in that daily walk? How does getting through the difficult sensations of hunger experienced during fasting—thus acquiring more discipline—possibly help you get through other rough patches in this area?

CHAPTER 9

WEEK 3—HEART V. STOMACH

VIRTUE OF THE WEEK: DISCIPLINE

This week's reading:

"By controlling what goes into our mouth and stomach we train ourselves to control what comes out of our mouth and heart. Through the discipline of fasting we may also control our eyes and avoid looking at things that will aggravate our passions further. Fasting also helps us learn to control our anger and, above all, manage our ego and pride, which are the main causes of our sinfulness.

According to St. John Chrysostom, fasting is to the soul what food is to the body; in the same way that material food nourishes our body, fasting strengthens the soul and makes its wings lighter and able to move more easily. Fasting helps lift the soul above this world to communicate uninhibited with the Creator, free from attachment to the pleasures and lusts of this life.

Rather, it offers spiritual medicine to cure our spiritual ills. It provides renewal, sanctification, and fortification when applied in conjunction with several other practices that help us heal, find peace and experience God's love. Repentance through the confession of sins is one of those practices needed along with fasting. Confession is the place and time where we humble ourselves and surrender to God's mercy. Through this act of humility we open up the heavens for the light of God to shine into our hearts and heal us. Forgiveness of others is also necessary, as we ask for God's forgiveness for our personal sins and try to find peace in our hearts."[1]

SUGGESTED AT-HOME ACTIVITY FOR THIS WEEK

Go out and remove the list nailed to your tree of choice and pick somewhere discreet to tear it up into little, tiny pieces. Once that is finished, once again write down your list of three sins and/or temptations on a little piece of paper along with your five personality characteristics of self-will. Now, find a little box of some kind, put the list in there, and hide the box somewhere nobody will ever find it! We are going to leave it there for the next two weeks and then it is going to get really exciting what we do next! (Don't read ahead . . . I know what you're thinking!)

---

1. Papageorgiou, "Fasting: Is It Really Necessary?" lines 28–38.

DAY 14, THURSDAY

Jesus said, "it is not what goes into the mouth that defiles a person, but what comes out of the mouth; this defiles a person . . . Do you not see that whatever goes into the mouth passes into the stomach and is expelled? But what comes out of the mouth proceeds from the heart and this defiles a person.

MATTHEW 11:17-18

This lesson from Jesus about the huge difference between what goes into the mouth, (namely food), and what comes out of it is extremely important to the Spirit of fasting because it teaches us the symbolic nature of food as well as its insignificance. Such a view of food matters a lot to us fasters because it shows us the proper place to keep food: one of humble insignificance. This is why when we fast we are simply using food as a representative of a much larger spiritual act. We are also fasting from the words, deeds, and thoughts of the heart that might keep us from growing closer to the Lord. By going without food, we are really striving to go without all those earthly temptations and more harmful desires of the flesh such as sexual immorality, love of money, hatred in relationships, hurtful words meant to inflict pain, etc. Obviously, food in itself is not a bad thing. It is very critical to get that point . . . food is symbolic; it is a physical manifestation of a spiritual reality. But it is not the culprit! Every natural food is a defining goodness from God and clean for all Christians. It is not the source of the problem, or sin in itself, or what makes a person bad. Rather, food acts as a spiritual medium—similar to what medium an artist chooses; like oil, watercolor, clay, or whatever to portray their art—that allows us to see beyond our earthly lives into other deeper aspects of our spiritual lives in heaven. Beyond this minute to minute capture of finite space lies our hearts, thoughts, and actions, in which food is merely a tangible medium to help us determine how we can come into closer, more constant communion with God, all that lies beyond in the Kingdom, and better able to identify what possibly may be keeping us from doing so. But it is usually, ultimately not food that is the problem at all, but all the other hindrances of character, emotion, and just plain being human that get in the way! Food just helps us become more conscious of what these problematic areas are, and as we give *it* up in hope that we can delve into the realm of the Spirit and give up those things to God as well. Or, if you're one of the extremely rare, yet extremely lucky few of us, then more able to avoid them all together to begin with!

Think back on those long lists of sins and temptations of the world as well as the long list of personality characteristics of self-will. Does it echo what Jesus has to say about what defiles a person? "But what comes out of the mouth proceeds from the heart, and this defiles a person. For out of the heart come evil thoughts, murder, adultery, sexual immorality, theft, false witness, slander. These are what defile a person" (Matthew 15: 18—20). Therefore, the mouth is just this great gateway of evil if what lies behind it (the heart) is full of malefaction. I picture the mouth as a great dam and the rivers of the heart the reservoir behind, which flows through. From the mouth come lies, cursing, abuse, and all kinds of badness. This is what needs to be gotten rid of, what needs to be *fasted* from. Abstaining from food just helps us as earthly beings learn how to gain the self-control to do this with all the unseen at the heart of the matter. The more we go without food and learn to fast for forty days like Jesus did in the wilderness, the more hopefully we will be able to go without all these other, deeper issues, that keep us from being One with his holiness.

- *Meditate for 10 minutes.* Blessed is he "whose delight is in the law of the LORD, and who *meditates* on his law day and night" (Psalm 1: 2).
- *Pray for 10 minutes.*
- *Enter All Data in Personal DRL.*

JOURNEY JOURNAL

Write down at least five other symbols found in the world . . . (i.e. the Shamrock symbolizes luck and good fortune, the red heart symbolizes love, the advent candle the four weeks of Christmas, etc.) How, in your own words, is food an example of symbolism in the Bible?

DAY 15, FRIDAY

In using spiritual weapons, "to fight the good fight, to walk the way of fasting, to crush the heads of the invisible dragons, to prove ourselves victorious over sin, and without condemnation to reach our goal of worshiping the Holy Resurrection."

—PRAYER OF THE PRESANCTIFIED LITURGY

Continuing the lesson from yesterday in that Jesus said what truly defiles a person is what comes out of their mouth because this flows from the heart, not what goes into a person's mouth. The differentiation here in what a fast should absolutely focus on here is crucial to understanding the meaning of fasting for purely spiritual reasons. The focus is not completely on food (although some has to be in order to do it all), but should mainly be on what comes *out* of our mouth since these thoughts, words, and deeds flow from the heart and this is what defiles a person. So, we should always be focused on fasting from sin, and what comes, out of our mouth. This can be accomplished by doing a physical abstinence from the food that goes into our mouth because it aids us in gaining self-control, discipline, knowledge of the self-will versus God's will, and many other valuable spiritual gifts. But fasting is not an end in itself, it is merely a spiritual weapon, or valuable tool in the set of armor to aid us in the human battle against sin; to help overcome the *invisible dragons* of sin and come out victorious, closer to Jesus in magnifying his resurrection.

I really like what one faster from the Greek Orthodox church had to say about the purposes of his fasting because it addresses the very point Jesus made about it being far more important what comes out of the mouth to the state of an individual's soul than what goes into the mouth. In his own words he said, "I think that this Lent I'm going to do my best to concentrate intensely on fasting from my thoughts, words and deeds . . . Asking myself why I think, say and do things . . . what reasoning or excuse do I have for thinking, saying, or doing things . . . and whether my thoughts, words and deeds are hurtful or beneficial to others and to myself. Most of all I must reflect on my thoughts, words, and deeds and ask if they bring Glory to Almighty God. If they don't then even my strictest fast in every form may be hypocritical. If they do, then the Easter Resurrection Service will bring an even deeper sense of joy in knowing that in some small way fasting brought my unworthy soul closer to God."[2] This follower of Christ demonstrates the

---

2. Demos, "Focus Fasting: A Reflection on the Great Fast," lines 13–16.

spirit of what Jesus meant when he said it is the thoughts and deeds of our heart, which then flow into the words from out of the mouth that truly have the power to defile, or perhaps, save a person. In other words, fasting by not eating food is not going to make you a better person, it is the lessons you learn through it about being in closer communion with Christ, and more in line with God's Word that ultimately does.

The material or physical reality of what goes into the mouth, food, is not nearly as significant as the greater spiritual significance of what comes out of it to a person's salvation and relationship with Jesus, and therefore God. However, abstinence from the physical, material food we put into our mouth powerfully helps us abstain from any evil sins that can live in the heart, thereby flowing out of the mouth in further defilement of the person. "First of all, fasting is abstinence from food. By detaching us from earthly goods and realities, fasting has a liberating effect on us and makes us worthy of the life of the spirit, a life similar to that of angels. Second, fasting as abstinence from bad habits and sin, is the mother of Christian virtues, the mother of sound and wholesome thinking; it allows us to establish the proper priority between the material and spiritual, giving priority to the spiritual."[3]

- *Meditate for 10 minutes.*
- *Pray for 10 minutes.*
- *Enter All Data in Personal DRL.*

---

3. Maximos, "On Fasting," lines 16–18.

JOURNEY JOURNAL

Write down any thoughts, feelings, or anything you want to communicate with the Lord about in the Journey Journal.

DAY 16, SATURDAY

Creative Space Page

Record any and everything you eat and at what exact time in the DRL. This is never an option. It is always mandatory and one of the 3 cardinal rules.

OCULI SUNDAY

"Eyes/Seeing"

Free Day!

Quick Friendly Reminder

Use this free time to learn to automatically better moderate your previous choices with the lessons you have gained from fasting. See it as a kind of special medium that coalesces how you normally ate and lived with what is now being integrated into this new way of eating and living. Sundays can be a wonderful opportunity to spiritually blend the old with the new to create a better mode of living with the risen Lord. Optional free writing opportunity available below!

JOURNEY JOURNAL

DAY 17, MONDAY

And the LORD said to Moses, "Write these words, for in accordance with these words I have made a covenant with you and with Israel." So he was there with the LORD forty days and forty nights. He neither ate bread nor drank water. And he wrote on the tablets the words of the covenant, the Ten Commandments.

EXODUS 34:27-28

The number forty is highly significant in the grand design of God's purposes and how he shows it to be performed on earth, as it is in heaven, throughout the Bible. The number forty demonstrates times God uses for his tests, hardships, trials, and ultimate judgments. It is also an extremely important number for fasting because it is repeated time and again throughout the Bible for this purpose exactly, and connects seemingly unrelated events together under God. That the number forty is explicitly prescribed to numerous events throughout Scripture of at first seemingly random events is indicative of God's ultimate purpose in his grand design for human history and how it is played out. The number forty connects all these biblical happenings into a bigger puzzle with the final picture formed being the purposes of God to demonstrate his wisdom, love, and judgment for creation. Such times of testing and hardship can be seen in the forty-days it rained on Noah before the flood (Genesis 7: 12), forty stripes is the maximum whipping penalty, the children of Israel put to the test wandering the wilderness for forty-years, (Hebrews 3: 9), the Philistine Goliath coming out every morning and evening for forty-days during the war with Saul challenging David to fight (1 Samuel 17: 16), and forty-weeks of pregnancy, just to name a few. God uses the number forty to represent a period of time that he tests and challenges his subjects in order to bring them into greater knowledge and understanding of his righteous judgments, unfailing love, and grace beyond all measure. He puts us to the test, in a time of intense trial, often seen repeatedly for forty-days, or forty-years, to reveal his complete power and sovereignty through all eternity. He controls the past, present, and future and the number forty is one of his chosen units of time to bring all things together into a greater message of truth.

Because the number forty is so important throughout Scripture, this entire week of Bible study is going to be devoted to showing you how and why. Hopefully it will encourage you to know that you are hardly alone in this forty-day-long fast, but that God appointed this very number of days to believers throughout history. It is a consecrated number, one set aside for holiness by the Creator. A designated time appointed for not just hardship, trial, and judgment; but *particularly* for fasting. First there was the divinely appointed fast of Jesus for forty-days in the wilderness, (Matt 4: 2), that we have already delved into earlier on. Then there was the forty-day fast of Moses before he received the Ten Commandments (34: 28). There was also the forty-day fast of Nineveh proclaimed through Jonah to avert God's judgment. Also, Elijah ate the miraculous food of angels, which gave him strength to last forty-days without eating any more food! (1 Kings 19: 8) The Israelites ate special Manna and quail from God himself for a partial fast in the wilderness lasting forty long years: "The people of Israel ate the manna forty-years, till they came to a habitable land. They ate the manna till they came to the border of the land of Canaan" (Exodus 16: 35). This week we are going to take an in depth look at each of these incredible examples of biblical fasting. As you can see, forty is a specially designated number appointed specifically for fasting throughout the Bible. It is used time and again as the prescribed period of time meant solely for this ancient spiritual activity—not only during Lent, however, throughout all time. That is how we are connected today to ancient biblical times and the early church—by this forty day long fast with the Savior— where others, alongside ourselves, also endured such periods of suffering and trial for the same amount of time. We are all connected in the Spirit of the Lord much more powerfully than we could even imagine when we are engaged forty-days in this discipline for the sake of his glory.

- *Meditate for 10 minutes.* "May these words of my mouth and this *meditation* of my heart be pleasing in your sight, LORD, my Rock and my Redeemer" (Psalm 19: 14).

- *Pray for 10 minutes.* Refer back to your list of prayer requests for specific people and the world at large. Try saying some aloud.

- *Enter All Data in Personal DRL.*

JOURNEY JOURNAL

Then I proclaimed a *fast* there, at the river Ahava, that we might humble ourselves before our God, to seek from him a safe journey for ourselves, our children and all our goods . . . So we *fasted* and implored our God for this, and he listened to our entreaty.

EZRA 8: 21, 23

Would you rather do a forty-day absolute fast like Moses and Jesus did or a forty-year long partial fast like the Israelites did, (with only quail meat in the evening and manna in the morning)? Why your choice?

DAY 18, TUESDAY

After fasting forty-days when he came down from Mount Sinai with the plaques of the Ten Commandments in hand, "Moses did not know that the skin of his face shone because he had been talking with God. Aaron and all the people of Israel saw Moses, and behold the skin of his face shone, and they were afraid to come near him.

EXODUS 34: 29-30

Moses went through an immense purification process when he fasted for forty days and forty nights when he received the great revelation of the Ten Commandments from God. It was as though fasting vastly aided and helped accomplish this incredible process of purification that the venerable Old Testament prophet had to go through in order to be holy enough to actually talk with the LORD God and receive them. This forty-day-long fast is the most miraculous event since it ends with Moses' face shining in a supernatural sense, as well as him receiving the divine law from God himself. He went up Mount Sinai, purifying his mind, body, and spirit in preparation to become the most pure vessel he possibly could be for the Lord to dwell in and reveal his glory. Moses communed with the LORD in a most blessed, sanctified state of supernatural power. Fasting dramatically helped magnify this power from within to allow for the LORD to more fully reveal the Divine to Moses. His shining face reminds me of the millions and millions of diamonds that shine so bright in the sun reflecting on freshly fallen snow. An unearthly, radiant light from above shone so brightly from the face of Moses that it scared the people who beheld it. Beyond a glow, it was so incredibly luminescent, this sacred light that appeared from his face. "This came about because Moses had reached the ultimate state of purification (catharsis), which allowed him to attain the state of illumination and finally become a dwelling place of the uncreated light of God (we call this transformation and unity with God *theosis*). Fasting was an essential element for Moses' purification as he approached Yahweh and stood in His presence. Ultimately, he was filled with the divine light."[4]

The overarching holy process of fasting forty days may be seen ultimately as a purification of sin. Sin that lives in the mind, body, and spirit can be easier washed away with the aid of this discipline properly done. Picture a car covered in mud from off-roading through the slums on Ash Wednesday. Next, envision a high- pressure hose spraying it with soap and

4. Papageorgiou, "Fasting: Is It Really Necessary?" lines 12-14.

water for forty-days until Easter Sunday. That car is going to be pretty sparkly clean as it rolls into the church parking lot Easter morning. Well, if the car is our soul and spirit, and the mud is the sin of the world that can get on it in varying degrees of defilement, then fasting is the high-pressured hose that sprays it off in a magical purification process until it is clean again. It is like the refiner's fire that purifies the specimen until it is holy, spotless, and without blame. Even someone as pious, reverent, and worthy as Moses, felt a need to perform this ancient spiritual discipline to help make himself ready to be a temple for the Lord. The fact that he did this and that the results were so magnificent—with the Ten Commandments recorded for all mankind—shows how powerful this old spiritual practice actually is. It is a carefully kept secret—a sacred, holy way to tap into the powers of the divine and have some of its radiant light shine in your own life. If someone as devout and faithful as Moses still felt a need and desire to further purify himself from sin, then all the more, do not we need to as well? So, go ahead, tap into the eternal fountain of life and feel more beautifully pure inside and out today as you fast for Christ. Feel more alive in him as we go on this enchanting journey towards wonder by wonder from this world into the one beyond.

- *Meditate for 10 minutes.* "My mouth will speak words of wisdom; the *meditation* of my heart will give you understanding" (Psalm 49: 3).
- *Pray for 10 minutes.*
- *Enter All Data in Personal DRL.*

JOURNEY JOURNAL

For he is like a refiner's fire and like fullers' soap. He will sit as a refiner and purifier of silver, and he will purify the sons of Levi and refine them like gold and silver, and they will bring offerings in righteousness to the LORD.

MALACHI 3:2-3

What are some other examples of purification processes that you can think of besides fasting and refining precious metals? How are the impurities (or sin as in the human case), found in these examples, "purified" out to reveal a final, finished product in its most perfect state?

DAY 19, WEDNESDAY

And the angel of the LORD came again in a second time and touched him and said, "Arise and eat, for the journey is too great for you." And he arose and ate and drank, and went in the strength of that food forty days and forty nights to Horeb, the mount of God.

1 KINGS 19:7-8

When first Elijah lay down under the broom tree, he was despairing of his life and implored the Lord to just take him away. "And he asked that he might die, saying, "It is enough; now, O LORD, take away my life, for I am no better than my fathers" (1 Kings 19: 4). Well, what happened between that moment when Elijah was near suicidal, he who would prefer rather to die than to go on living, and the strong prophet, whose name means 'My God is Yaweh'—being able to accomplish an arduous forty day and forty night journey to Mount Horeb? Not to mention that on his whole trip to Mt. Horeb he had no more to eat than but what the angel had given him to eat. No, he went in the sustenance of that magical food the entire, arduous way to the destined mountain without eating anything else. In other words, that angelic, celestial food from heaven had the power to give him strength and tide Elijah over unlike anything else we can compare. It must have been some kind of incredible food the angel of the LORD gave him! What could we compare it to? Energy bars? Luckily, we know exactly what it was . . . For after he lay down and slept once again under the broom tree—famished, depleted, exhausted after all his running from Ahab—"behold, an angel touched him and said to him, "Arise and eat." And he looked, and behold, there was at his head a cake baked on hot stones and a jar of water. And he ate and drank and lay down again" (1 Kings 19: 5–6). Wow! What incredibly magical food, sent from heaven, with cake baked on stone and fresh water that appears! And best of all, if one eats and drinks of it as Elijah did, then it has the divine power to give strength to the body for forty days and forty nights of fasting with nothing else being eaten. Please, God, give me some of this blessed food!

So, Elijah was given a special food from God that allowed him to not only fast forty days and forty nights, but also to go on fasting without consuming *any food* while completing an arduous, physical journey to Mount Horeb. He would have been expending great physical energy and exertions to complete this trek that took forty days; yet Elijah did it without having to eat the entire time! The magical strength God gave him in that angelic food presented under the broom tree was enough to sustain the prophet. It is through the forty days of fasting done by Elijah that we can learn to trust and depend entirely on God for our sustenance, wellbeing, and every need. We need not worry about what we will eat or drink or how we will get there. All we need to do is completely trust that our Father will take care us as he always has and always will for our every need. Doing a forty-day-long fast—similar to Elijah, and other examples we have been and will continue to look at in the Bible—teaches us to give up resorting to ourselves and the fallacy of self-reliance . . . and rather to give up the self. It teaches us to give up our self-will, security in material things and our time—to give all this over to God in complete dependence and trust. We learn through fasting to depend on God for when and how we shall eat, and at what times (if at all), and to fill our spirits with sustaining power to get through the difficult times of discomfort and uncertainty. Our Father fills our bodies as vessels with a greater spirit of the LORD that readily gets us through days of possible hunger as we trust and depend on him entirely to do just that. Elijah did not question whether he would be able to make that forty-day journey without food, but faithfully marched forth in the strength of that spiritual food of angels, and so can we! Let us pull up our bootstraps, set our eyes on the Lord, and keep those chins up and be more like Elijah in fasting biblically!

- *Meditate for 10 minutes*, preferably outside. Lent comes from the old English word "lengthen" which is what the days do in the springtime, so meditation should be much nicer and also more elevating out of doors. Open the ears to the sound of birds and just dwell in light with the serenity of the spirit.
- *Pray for 10 minutes.*
- *Enter All Data in Personal DRL.*

JOURNEY JOURNAL

Write down anything you may want or need to communicate with the Father about in the Journey Journal. Remember, nothing is too small or too big for Our Father, and he does truly care about it all even if that's hard to believe sometimes.

    Blessed are those whose lawless deeds are forgiven, and whose sins are covered; blessed is the man against whom the Lord will not count his sin.
    Romans 4:7–8

CHAPTER 10

WEEK 4—THE NUMBER 40

VIRTUE OF THE WEEK: PURITY

This week's reading:

"Let each one of us keep in mind the benefit of fasting . . . For this healer of our souls is effective, in the case of one to quieten the fevers and impulses of the flesh, in another to assuage bad temper, in yet another to drive away sleep, in another to stir up zeal, and in yet another to restore purity of mind and to set him free from evil thoughts. In one it will control his unbridled tongue, and, as it were by a bit, restrain it by the fear of God and prevent it from uttering idle and corrupt words. In another it will invisibly guard his eyes and fix them on high instead of allowing them to roam hither and thither, and thus cause him to look on himself and teach him to be mindful of his own faults and shortcomings. Fasting gradually disperses and drives away spiritual darkness and the veil of sin that lies on the soul, just as the sun dispels the mist. Fasting enables us spiritually to see that spiritual air in which Christ, the Sun who knows no setting, does not rise, but shines without ceasing. Fasting, aided by vigil, penetrates and softens hardness of heart, where once were the vapors of drunkenness it causes fountains of compunction to spring forth. I beseech you, brethren, let each of us strive that this may happen in us! Once this happens we shall readily, with God's help, cleave through the whole sea of passions and pass through the waves of the temptations inflicted by the cruel tyrant, and so come to anchor in the port of impassibility.

'My brethren, it is not possible for these things to come about in one day or one week! They will take much time, labor, and pain, in accordance with each man's attitude and willingness, according to the measure of faith and one's contempt for the objects of sight and thought. In addition, it is also in accordance with the fervor of his ceaseless penitence and its constant working in the secret chamber of his heart that this is accomplished more quickly or more slowly by the gift and grace of God. But without fasting no one was ever able to achieve any of these virtues or any others, *for fasting is the beginning and foundation of every spiritual activity.*'[1]

SUGGESTED AT-HOME ACTIVITY FOR THIS WEEK

Pick out two different objects, such as pennies, grains of rice, or whatever you can find that is small and count it out to forty. Count it in a line with one object—like a long train with forty carts—and then form it into a pile with the other object. All the while let your mind meditate on the number forty and its significance to you during this fast. Then, once you have forty objects counted out choose a vessel to put them into. Contemplate how you are like that vessel, containing the spirit of fasting for forty days, and how great that is!

---

1. St Symeon, *Sayings On Fasting, the Discourses,*" lines 1–12.

DAY 20, THURSDAY

The people of Israel ate the manna forty years till they came to a habitable land. They ate the manna till they came to the border of the land of Canaan.

EXODUS 16:35

The people of Israel ate bread from heaven for forty years while they went through the wilderness on their journey to the land promised them. Again, there is the holy number forty designated for a time of fasting and complete reliance on God. Unlike Moses, Jesus, and Elijah who went forty days without eating food, which is known as an absolute fast; a partial fast is where you still do eat food but go for periods of time in total abstinence, or only eat certain types of food. (We also made this key differentiation in types of fasting in John the Baptist at the very beginning). Theirs was a partial fast, since they still ate the food God provided them in the evening and the morning. Ours is a partial fast too, but we only eat in the evening, and it's for forty days, not forty years, (thank goodness)! What was this mystical food sent down from heaven to the Israelites? Similar to how Elijah received the spiritual food from the angel of the Lord, this sustenance was also delivered divinely. "In the evening quail came up and covered the camp, and in the morning dew lay around the camp. And when the dew had gone up, there was on the face of the wilderness a fine, flake-like thing, fine as frost on the ground ... Now the house of Israel called its name manna. It was like coriander seed, white, and the taste of it was like wafers made with honey" (Exodus 16: 13–14, 31). And this is all they had to eat for forty years, relying solely on the LORD for their survival needs. This lesson teaches us to put our faith, trust, and total dependence in the Lord. We are his children, and he our Shepherd. And just like children must depend on their parents to take care of them, so does our loving Father, desire this trusting relationship with us.

The people of Israel were in a helpless condition when they started grumbling about being hungry, and that they would have rather died at the hands of the Egyptians than be led into utter desolation in the wilderness by Moses and Aaron. This condition of helplessness is exactly what the LORD God wants us to realize about our humble state. We can do nothing on our own, but must admit our helplessness and powerlessness. In a spirit of surrender and supplication, we cry out for our desperate need for Jehovah, which he listens to and always delivers. He wants us to realize how much we need him for everything, not just food, and to trust in him entirely. This is how faith is tested, proven, and built up stronger. The people of Israel learned to be obedient to the Word by learning to be totally dependent on God for their daily bread and sustenance. If we can endure to learn to put total trust in him, then he will take care of our every need. We must seek him in prayer and put greater faith in this promise and not rely on ourselves, our possessions, or other people to do this instead. Food is only a primal, basic need, but we need much, much more to be fulfilled as human beings. Fasting is an expression of showing our helplessness to God in that we need him to fulfill our greater spiritual needs. It is a humble act that surrenders the self to his greater will for our salvation, our purification from sin, our love of life, and ultimate freedom to live in grace.

- *Meditate for 10 minutes*, preferably outside.
- *Pray for 10 minutes*. Mostly I speak out loud my prayers to God, but sometimes I do not pray out loud. I find that saying the words out loud is a very effective form of praying. It helps to keep the praise and requests specific when audible and is what we do at church and bible study.
- *Enter All Data in Personal DRL.*

JOURNEY JOURNAL

Write down at least three other needs, besides food, you have that only the Father can deliver. How can fasting help us to realize our other, greater, truer needs?

DAY 21, FRIDAY

Jonah began to go into the city, going a day's journey. And he called out, "yet forty days, and Nineveh shall be overthrown!" And the people of Nineveh believed God. They called for a fast and put on sackcloth, from the greatest of them to the least of them.

JONAH 3:4-5

Once again, the magical number forty is prescribed as a biblical account of fasting for God. Why did Jonah say precisely forty days instead of say, thirty, or twenty-five? Because the awesome God of the universe further revealed his truth and ultimate purpose for connecting seemingly unrelated events into his grand design for humanity. Like connecting the random dots on a very sophisticated map of the history of mankind, are these periodic forty-day fasts related throughout the Bible. God slowly unveils a master plan as we, the fasters, painstakingly connect the dots to reveal a beautiful, individual portrait unique to each of our lives and trust it fits into the bigger scheme. The fasting done by the people of Nineveh is but yet another echo of the forty-day Lenten fast. At first glance, the two seemingly unrelated events are similar in many other ways besides lasting for the exact same number of days . . . The fasting is done for the purpose of humbling oneself—as seen in the sackcloth—and coming before the LORD God in repentance for one's sins, in the hope of eternal salvation.

The whole reason the people of Nineveh called a fast for forty days was to show true, humble repentance for their vileness, which had brought judgment upon the city. By reducing themselves to a humble state of human hunger, clothed in paltry rags, they appealed to God's great mercy in proclaiming he the all-powerful master and they the weak and helpless to his wrathful, almighty hand. In essence, such dutiful submission is a graphic display of faith, hope, and complete belief in the powers that reign. It shows a submission of the self will to the will of God in knowledge that he is the one in control, not us, and to prove it . . . we will fast. The king of Nineveh issued the following decree: "Let neither man nor beast, herd nor flock, taste anything. Let them not feed or drink water, but let man and beast be covered with sackcloth, and let them call out mightily to God. Let everyone turn from his evil way and from the violence that is in his hands" (Jonah 3: 7–8).

Does not this call to the people of Nineveh resound in our own hearts this Lent season? Are there not things we need to turn away from and renounce to the true God, or at least work to improve in ourselves? Now, I'm not telling you to starve your puppy or kitten, but I am telling you there is an important connection between these two events in the greater purposes that God has for his people—and fasting as a whole. During Lent, similar to the cry of the King of Nineveh, we also turn away from our wicked, worldly ways, and humbly admit our sins before the Lord in an effort to avert judgment and obtain forgiving mercy. By fasting, we too, like people of Nineveh, humble ourselves, (for me sackcloth consists of sweatpants and not getting ready much), and refrain from personal pleasures and comforts in the material (i.e. food), in an effort to cleanse the spiritual soul of anything keeping us from unity with Christ. We give up those things, which are wrong in the eyes of the Lord, so that we may stay in God's everlasting mercy, grace, and peace. Well, God rewarded the people of Nineveh greatly for their fasting in not bringing their city to ruin—and he will reward us too! There is a direct, tangible result and many rich rewards for such commitment to holiness. How does having a mighty spiritual weapon to battle the forces of evil sound? Well, the art of fasting is exactly that in a nutshell. How these results and rewards manifest in real life are understood and felt differently from individual to individual, as part of each one's unique relationship and journey with Christ. But Jesus does always answer and transform according to the measure of our openness and willingness for him to enact such undeserved grace.

- *Meditate for 10 minutes*, preferably outside.
- *Pray for 10 minutes.*
- *Enter All Data in Personal DRL.*

JOURNEY JOURNAL

If you abide in me, and my words abide in you, ask whatever you wish, and it will be done for you. By this my Father is glorified, that you bear much fruit and so prove to be my disciples.

JOHN 15:7-8

Write down any questions you might have so far in the fasting journey. Can you relate with the people of Nineveh? Why or why not?

DAY 22, SATURDAY

Creative Space Page

Record *any* and *everything* you eat and at what exact time in the DRL. This is never an option. It is always mandatory and one of the 3 cardinal rules.

LAETARE OR MOTHERING SUNDAY

"Celebration/Rejoice"

Free Day

JOURNEY JOURNAL

For God alone my soul waits in silence; from him comes my salvation. He alone is my rock and my salvation, my fortress; I shall not be greatly shaken.

PSALM 62:1-2

DAY 23, MONDAY

And after fasting forty days and forty nights, he was hungry. And the tempter came and said to him, "If you are the Son of God, command these stones to become loaves of bread." But he answered, "It is written, 'Man shall not live by bread alone, but by every word that comes from the mouth of God.'"

MATTHEW 4:2-4

These are probably the single, most important words we have on fasting in all of the history of literature. Embodied within this immortal response from Jesus is wisdom for the ages. He said this after fasting forty days to the great tempter, the Devil. Within these words are instructions to keep in mind not only during fasting and for the power to overcome sin, but for how to live all of life. It conveys the message that mankind needs much, much more than mere food alone to live meaningful lives. Bread to fill the stomach is only the first, most basic need of man and even all the beasts of the field do this. Jesus is saying that men (and women) cannot be truly satisfied or completely fulfilled by just the mere meeting of this basic need each day. We need vastly more to make us happy, to fill us spiritually, to make us whole. Bread, or whatever other manner of tasty food, cannot fill us with what we as humans truly need and want. To be in closer communion with God, to live meaningful and productive lives of service helping others, to love and be loved in return, to be filled with the Spirit of the Lord, to learn wisdom and truth, and to be happy in heart, mind, and body, is what we truly want and what Jesus desires for us. Mere food cannot accomplish any of this for us! Only by being obedient and understanding the Word of God, can any of these gifts of eternal life be produced in us. By reading the Bible, and absorbing each precious word that came out of Jesus' lips, we can fully, truly ingest the life-saving fruits of peace, love, happiness, humility, discipline, kindness, patience, self-control . . . well, the list of blessings goes on and on. Only then can we take these immense blessings and apply them to our lives in the world.

The great richness of blessings is found in Christ alone. All we have to do is seek him, accept that he is Truth, and give our sin(s) over to him to be forgiven and cleansed so that we may live in peace with God. The reward is having every spiritual need met here on earth—something far more valuable than the momentary gratification that comes from ice cream or cheeseburgers. The rewards are truly endless when we set our hearts, minds, and bodily focus on what Jesus said, on who he was, and every word that comes from the mouth of God. Do not settle for the short-lived, transitory reward food or other fleeting material objects offer for they do not last, nor can they make you truly happy or full of peace. Rather, give up these material temptations of food, drink, material goods, and whatever else keeps the soul from experiencing true joy, light, love, and wellbeing in the Lord. His words alone have the ability to fill us spiritually with what we need to live life fully and richly, which nothing as common or insubstantial as food or other material things have the power to do. Put your hope in what is eternal—the Word of God—and you will be richly blessed, full of the long-lasting, durable rewards of peace, wisdom, and spiritual experiences beyond your wildest dreams. Real pleasure will flood your being from a difficult job well done because you had the strength of grace, or a true victory felt which lasts and lasts, instead of the quick pleasure that fades from a tasty meal or recently bought purchase.

- *Meditate for 10 minutes*, preferably outside. Tune out all distractions and return to the breath of life that connects you to the Creator all living things. If and when an intrusive thought or bit of stress comes, intentionally let it go, relax deeper into the complete stillness of unmoving peace.
- *Pray for 10 minutes.*
- *Enter All Data in Personal DRL.*

JOURNEY JOURNAL

Blessed is the one who finds wisdom, and the one who gets understanding, for the gain from her is better than gain from silver and her profit better than gold. She is more precious than jewels, and nothing you desire can compare with her. Long life is in her right hand; in her left hand are riches and honor. Her ways are ways of pleasantness, and all her paths are peace. She is a tree of life to those who lay hold of her; those who hold her fast are called blessed.

PROVERBS 3:13–18

Write about at least five other blessings that you already have and may be trying to grow. Now write about five other blessings that you do not have yet hope for. Compare the lasting quality of these more important desires to the quickly digested and disposed of quality of food and the differences in the pleasure they bring.

DAY 24, TUESDAY

Do not work for the food that perishes, but for the food that endures to eternal life, which the Son of Man will give to you.

JOHN 6:27

All of the food that we eat or do not eat each day is perishable. It has a very real shelf life. And when we put it into our body it is simply digested and excreted. No matter how fancy or expensive the lunch may be, or how delicious, it all just comes out as poop in the end anyways, right? This is the way of all perishable food, for all species. There is nothing special about it. It is always the same. However, Jesus has another kind of food that is different, that is exciting, and that is magical. It is a kind of food that does not perish but lasts forever. The Savior is the keeper of this very, very special kind of food that is altogether better than any regular food we could work for or eat. Imagine, a food right now in your kitchen that would last forever (besides Wonder bread)! This supernatural substance that the Lord has to give us, to feed us with, is supernatural in nature, it is "spiritual food." Right here, he makes a clear distinction between ordinary food and this spiritual food that he has to offer. He also says that the special kind he has to offer is far superior to ordinary food and that we should seek it instead of the mundane, everyday kinds that perish. So, let us not eat, but fast for a period of time while contemplating the extraordinariness of this mysterious food.

The crowd then asked him, "What must we do, to be doing the works of God?" Jesus answered them, "This is the work of God, that you believe in him whom he has sent." (John 6: 28–29) Sounds easy right? But wait . . . here is a supernatural, divine deity filled with the power of God that can raise people from the dead, give you food that makes you live forever, will die for the sake of your sins, be gentle in the face of prosecution and teach us to love our enemies, and walk forty days himself after rising from the dead. Still sound easy to believe? All of who he is and what he did here on earth was beyond the typical scope of human comprehension. Yet we can and do believe all of this because we have faith. Faith allows us to know what is true without having to see it at all. We live by it in the most spiritual sense, and not by physical sight alone. Faith believes the impossible with the hope, wonder, and acceptance of a child. Without question, these beliefs, allow us to live in the miraculous realm of the Spirit and see everything in a whole new way. The first step is surrender and acceptance that Christ is the Living Truth, the Son of the one and only true God, and that he was sent by the Father to do his miraculous work. The next step is to believe and know that God dwelt fully in Christ and the two are One by the Holy Spirit. Then, believe all the miracles and divine events in the Bible with complete faith and you're set. Nothing about it is easy to believe; even that there is this paranormal food that is imperishable that lasts eternally. All we have to do though as believers, is truly, absolutely, and without fear *believe*. Surrender what society, science, and other people may argue about what logic and what truth and reality may be and accept that Jesus was God incarnate and saved us sinners from a wrathful eternity of hell separated from the Father. Because he died on the cross and suffered we can have this eternal life and live forever, through him, who is the imperishable food, the bread of heaven. All we must do is simply believe that he was sent from God and died on the cross for our sins so that we could have peace with God now and in the afterlife. There is one slight caveat which part of Lent is devoted to . . . because he did all this for us, we need to repent of our sins and give them over to him so that he can truly forgive us. We must not go on sinning, "as a dog returns to his vomit, so a fool repeats his folly," (Proverbs 26: 11), or we make a mockery of his death and resurrection. We need to learn from our mistakes and accept the grace of his amazing forgiveness so that we can live redeemed as free Christians. All we must do to earn this undeserved state of earthly happiness—free from sin and pure—is to believe that Jesus can totally remove our dirty sin or bad habits from us, which he unconditionally does. Only then can we live a life more free from problems, stress, anxiety, worry, and all kinds of dark complications. This he does out of love for us and is the whole reason he came to earth, so we better let him do it without hindrance!

- *Meditate for 10 minutes.* Be filled with the spirit of healing in soothing, relaxing calm. Perhaps listen to some lovely, nature music to help inspire this mood of healing.
- *Pray for 10 minutes.*
- *Enter All Data in Personal DRL.*

JOURNEY JOURNAL

For I will forgive their wickedness and I will remember their sins no more.
HEBREWS 8:12

Why is it sometimes harder for us, as people, to forgive ourselves for sins or harmful mistakes when God is not only able to do this, but also to completely forget about it? Is it easier for you to forgive others for their trespasses against you, or easier to forgive yourself for bad mistakes or things you have done? Record why you think that is in the Journey Journal.

DAY 25, WEDNESDAY

The crowd said, "Our fathers ate the manna in the wilderness; as it is written, 'He gave them bread from heaven to eat.' Jesus then said to them, "Truly, truly, I say to you, it was not Moses who gave you the bread from heaven, but my Father gives you the true bread from heaven. For the bread of God is he who comes down from heaven and gives life to the world."

JOHN 6:31-34

The most important phrase in this scripture is, in my humble opinion, is *'the bread of God.'* It is so paramount to understand what this is referring to in comparison to the other *bread of heaven*, that the Israelites ate for forty years in the wilderness. The one is spiritual food, heavenly sent, and the other is Jesus Christ. Our Father in heaven sent his only, beloved Son to earth, as bread to feed the masses for his good pleasure. He gave his precious Son, Jesus, as a great, delicious loaf of everlasting bread that could sustain, and give nourishing life to the people of the world. This miraculous food, (bread), that God gave to us to be fed with eternally, is the actual divine body of Jesus Christ in the flesh. That is why "Jesus said to them, "I am the bread of life; whoever comes to me shall not hunger, and whoever believes in me shall never thirst" (John 6: 35). Then, this bread that our Creator gives us to eat and be forever satisfied by is no other than our Lord who died on the cross. We should eat more of this bread of God everyday in the form of learning and loving more about Jesus, and becoming as much like him as possible. Rather than being satisfied with mere perishable food, we need to seek the "true bread from heaven" and follow after our Lord in steadfast love. We need to seek Christ for the answers and in time of trouble because he is the comforting nourishment of the soul.

The bread that came down from heaven to the Israelites in the wilderness was spiritual food, but it was still perishable. Even Moses warned them not to leave it overnight lest it rot, which they did anyways. This manna is similar to the spiritual food given to Elijah from the angel that kept him in strength forty days, in the form of a cake baked on stone, in that they are both heaven sent. However, these excellent examples we are given in the Old Testament are just that . . . old illustrations relating to the ancient law, that was replaced by the coming of the New covenant of Christ. That is why the manna, even though true it was sent from heaven to the children of Israel, is not the "bread of God" itself. No, it was a lesser form of spiritual food supplied by God for a time, but not the most miraculous form of bread that was yet to be revealed for humanity's salvation. Manna was older, antiquated bread from heaven that directly symbolizes the Old Law of Moses that was to be replaced by a new, better law built on Spirit, brotherly love, grace, and faith by the new, truer bread of heaven—Christ. Jesus once said, "Truly, truly, I say to you, whoever believes in me has eternal life. I am the bread of life. Your fathers ate the manna in the wilderness, and they died. This is the bread that comes down from heaven, so that one may eat of it and not die" (John 6: 47–50). All we have to do is to believe, and have faith in Jesus Christ, and he will raise us up so that we may live forever! He is the eternal life, and the only way to life after death. Without him our souls would die and perish as the perishable food in the cupboard, but with faith in Christ our souls can be eternally fed by the real, everlasting bread in heaven.

- *Meditate for 10 minutes.* "May my meditation be pleasing to him, as I rejoice in the LORD" (Psalm 104: 34).
- *Pray for 10 minutes.*
- *Enter All Data in Personal DRL.*

JOURNEY JOURNAL

Write down anything you may want to communicate to your Father in the Journey Journal.

CHAPTER 11

WEEK 5—SYMBOLIC NATURE OF FOOD

VIRTUES OF THE WEEK: TEMPERANCE & MODERATION

This week's reading:

> The house of Jacob asking of the LORD God; "'Why have we fasted, and you see it not? Why have we humbled ourselves, and you take no knowledge of it?'

"Behold, in the day of your fast you seek your own pleasure, and oppress all your workers. Behold, you fast only to quarrel and to fight and to hit with a wicked fist. Fasting like yours this day will not make your voice to be heard on high. Is such the fast that I choose, a day for a person to humble himself? Is it to bow down his head like a reed, and to spread sackcloth and ashes under him? Will you call this a fast, and a day acceptable to the Lord?

> "Is not this the fast that I choose: to loose the bonds of wickedness, to undo the straps of the yoke, to let the oppressed go free, and to break every yoke? Is it not to share your bread with the hungry and bring the homeless poor into your house; when you see the naked, to cover him, and not to hide yourself from your own flesh? Then shall your light break forth like the dawn, and your healing shall spring up speedily; your righteousness shall go before you; the glory of the LORD shall be your rear guard. Then you shall call, and the LORD will answer; you shall cry, and he will say, 'Here I am.' If you take away the yoke from your midst, the pointing of the finger, and speaking wickedness,

if you pour yourself out for the hungry and satisfy the desire of the afflicted, then shall your light rise in the darkness and your gloom be as the noonday. And the LORD will guide you continually and satisfy your desire in scorched places and make your bones strong; and you shall be like a watered garden, like a spring of water, whose waters do not fail. And your ancient ruins shall be rebuilt; and you shall raise up the foundations of many generations; and shall be called the repairer of the breach, the restorer of streets to dwell in" (Isaiah 58: 3–12).

SUGGESTED AT-HOME ACTIVITY THIS

Go retrieve your hidden box from wherever it is (hopefully you didn't forget where it is), with the piece of paper inside . . . There are a number of ways to perform the following ceremony: you can come quietly to church by yourself sometime with your little box in hand. Sit quietly before the altar in the sanctuary and when you are ready, bring forth your box and set it on the altar before the Lord as you literally give your sins, temptations, and defects over to the Lord. Another way to do this ceremony is to have the person who actually leads this bible study perform the act of taking each of your boxes and placing them on the altar to be given over to the Lord in humble repentance. Leave it there, on the altar, for at least ten to fifteen minutes while you commune with the Lord. When you feel the power of the ceremony has succeeded take back your box and throw the paper away that was inside—once and for all.

DAY 26, THURSDAY

So Jesus said to them, "Truly, truly, I say to you, unless you eat the flesh of the Son of Man and drink his blood, you have no life in you. Whoever feeds on my flesh and drinks my blood has eternal life, and I will raise him up on the last day. For my flesh is true food, and my blood is true drink.

JOHN 6: 53-55

So how do we feed on the flesh of Christ and drink of His blood? It is through the taking of Holy Communion that we do this as we remember his death and resurrection. Through his blood we are forgiven our sins, but we must first repent and give them over to him completely so that we can be totally freed. Then, when we take the little piece of bread that is symbolic of the flesh of the body of Christ, we take it into our bodies. Then, as we drink from the holy chalice that holds the wine (or grape juice), it is symbolic of his blood that he spilt on the cross for our sins. The wine and bread taken at Communion is the spiritual reality of the fact that we as Christians are symbolically drinking the blood of Christ and symbolically eating his flesh. For although the wine and bread are purely symbolic of his actual blood and flesh, Jesus himself sanctioned this eating of bread, and drinking of wine, in remembrance of him so by his words there is a supernatural power given to communion. Because the bread and wine were spoken by Jesus to symbolically represent his body and blood for eternity, we are to do this until Christ returns. He sanctioned Communion to deliver this actual, true spiritual power of his real body and blood into ordinary bread and wine for believers in ages to come. "While they were eating, Jesus took bread, and when he had given thanks, he broke it and gave it to his disciples, saying, "Take and eat; this is my body." Then he took a cup, and when he had given thanks he gave it to them, saying, "Drink from it, all of you. This is my blood of the covenant, which is poured out for many for the forgiveness of sins" (Matthew 26: 26-28).

Well, how is this relevant to fasting for Great Lent? In many ways, dear friend! Through this most powerful, original symbolism of food being the body of Christ, we can learn how to view all food in this divine light. The more we learn about Jesus and what he meant by saying he was the bread come down from heaven, the more we can see any ordinary food as symbolic of a far greater spiritual reality. As we fast from "food" we allow all food to be symbolic in nature, in that we are truly fasting from sin, bad habits, undesirable thoughts, words, and deeds, and anything else that separates us from better knowing Christ. As we literally abstain from placing food in our mouth all day long, everyday, for forty days, we spiritually try to abstain, or better understand, what other harmful, wrong, bad sinful habits or personality characteristics we need to get rid of. Lent fasting is a great spiritual journey of discovering what else in our lives needs to be completely cast out, thrown away, and wiped off the face of the planet. Food is merely the physical gateway that allows us to walk under its arch to peer into our own heart, lives, spiritual realities, and mind. In going without the symbolic reality of food, we also show a desire to God to go without the rest of the unnecessary baggage in our lives that keeps us further from him and experiencing the fullness of his grace, and a willingness to give it up to him. As we daily abstain, we show this earnest desire to be purified and draw closer to Him in faithful action—shown most powerfully in the more difficult nature of non-action from eating food.

- *Meditate for 10 minutes*, preferably outside. Visualize the unmoving nature of statues, trees, and the structure of building all around as you become part of that archaic, permanent stillness in body and thought.
- *Pray for 10 minutes.*
- *Enter All Data in Personal DRL.*

JOURNEY JOURNAL

But if we walk in the light, as he is in the light, we have fellowship with one another, and the blood of Jesus, his Son, purifies us from all sin.

1 JOHN 1: 7

Write about how fasting from food may help you "fast" from other things. Do you find yourself more focused and more able to see these spiritual things? Or maybe more disciplined to have greater self-control so you can realize better what you are doing from moment to moment and more aware what else you may need to abstain from?

DAY 27, FRIDAY—TEMPERANCE & MODERATION

Every athlete exercises self-control in all things. They do it to receive a perishable wreath, but we an imperishable. So I do not run aimlessly; I do not box as one beating the air. But I discipline my body and keep it under control, lest after preaching to others I myself should be disqualified.

1 CORINTHIANS 9:25-27

Whenever we abstain from giving in to the temptation to eat, and abstain from food for long periods of time, we are exercising self-control. The more we do this, the more the virtue of self-control is cultivated within us. No longer do hands aimlessly reach for cookies or junk food during daylight hours . . . the spirit quietly slaps those hands to be obedient and wait for that one modest meal later in the evening. Fasting is very similar to an athletic discipline such as running, swimming, or skiing. Except instead of learning to control and exercise our physical bodies for a perishable prize, we are learning to control and exercise our total mind, body, and spirit in accordance with the Holy Spirit for an imperishable one. Still, fasting does take formidable self-control of the body itself, with its appetites, just as any athletic discipline. It is an elevated spiritual activity, which requires great resolve, to deny the typical pleasures and comforts of the flesh in exchange for the immortal gifts. From self-control comes discipline, from discipline temperance, from temperance moderation in all things, which results in better living year after year. What if I told you that through diligent fasting you would be able to have near complete financial control and resist overspending or impulsive purchases? Well, it is true. What if I told you that you would be able to control your emotions better, enabling you to moderate those harsh words, or overreactions, into a nice, easy calm? Well, it is true.

Through diligent fasting one learns to be satisfied and content with what one has, or a little, rather than constantly seeking more. There is finally an end to the unquenchable cravings of the flesh, as certain rules are set to temper it down. The limits set in the rules of the fast, help us develop the self-control to live within these. We have to strictly limit the amount of food we are allowed to eat, and what kind, and so living within these boundaries teaches us how to do so virtuously. Moderation, self-control and temperance naturally come as gifts of the spirit to the one who follows the rules. These incredible virtues can then be applied to all areas of life at large and truly facilitate change in other areas, if necessary.

Society has always told us bigger is better, more is desirable. Do not be satisfied with your current phone or car but constantly be seeking the next best thing because newer is better, and more and more money is the point of life, right? There are no rules to limit consumption, yet instead the exact opposite is encouraged by society: excess, greed, constantly without end. It is not okay to just be content with who you are in yourself, in Christ; you have to constantly be showing off your indulgences in the greater pleasures of life and flaunting your excessive riches for people to see. Otherwise, you are nobody. Perhaps being nobody to the world, you should rejoice, by being a crucial somebody to the Lord, which is the most important. By fasting, we gain the ability to apply moderation to all things . . . how much money we spend, how much frivolous things we do, how much we hang out with friends, etc. A great and most wonderful balance to life as a whole is produced as some of the fruits bloom from days spent well. What started as the seed of moderation, temperance, and self-control in regards to food while fasting, spreads to the learned ability to moderate all things in life as the spirit manifests itself. Self-control in regards to other things, like yelling, gossip, overspending, drinking too much alcohol, working too much, spending too much time with certain people, and other potentially harmful excesses is now more possible. Overall, temperance settles in like a cool and faithful breeze that promises to always blow at hot times. There exists a newfound level of contentment as one finally learns to just be content with a little that is healthy goodness, and with what one has, rather than be always wanting more. The actual need is greater union with Christ, and not more food or anything else material. As these other distractions are limited we are able to tap into the wealth of resources inside each of us in the Kingdom of heaven, which leaves us more contented than ever thought possible.

- *Meditate for 10 minutes*, preferably outside. "Do not let your adorning be external— the braiding of hair and the putting on of gold jewelry, or the clothing you wear—but let your adorning be the hidden person of the heart with the imperishable beauty of a gentle and quiet spirit, which in God's sight is very precious" (Peter 3: 3-4).
- *Pray for 10 minutes.*
- *Enter All Data in Personal DRL.*

JOURNEY JOURNAL

Better a patient person than a warrior, one with self-control than one who takes a city.

PROVERBS 16:32

What are some other excesses that it would benefit you spiritually to work on limiting in your life? Similar to food, these may be just, simple, common everyday goods and things that in too much excess can turn sour. Remember the saying; "too much of a good thing," and how this could apply to other things (or people) in your life that need new rules or limitations.

DAY 28, SATURDAY

Creative Space Page

Record *any* and *everything* you eat and at what exact time in the DRL. This is never an option. It is always mandatory and one of the 3 cardinal rules.

PASSION SUNDAY
Free Day

JOURNEY JOURNAL

Wait for the Lord and keep his way, and he will exalt you to inherit the land; you will look on when the wicked are cut off.

PSALM 37:34

DAY 29, MONDAY

Whoever feeds on my flesh and drinks my blood abides in me, and I in him. As the living Father sent me, and I live because of the Father, so whoever feeds on me, he also will live because of me. This is the bread that came down from heaven, not like the bread the fathers ate, and died. Whoever feeds on this bread will live forever.

JOHN 6: 54-58

Remember from last week that the feeding on Christ's flesh was the bread taken in Holy Communion and the drinking of His blood symbolized in the wine drunk thereof. Now, an extremely important point that he makes in regards to what happens when we do this spiritual act of Communion is summed up in six or seven words: *abides in me, and I in him.* These eternal words are so incredibly crucial, so poignant, that to miss them would be not only easy to do, but also tragic. It is the absolute key to understanding the New Testament gospel and how Jesus dwells in us, and we in him, and how the power and magic of the Holy Spirit takes place! Our Savior spiritually enters our body whenever we take of the spiritual bread of his body, and the spiritual wine of his blood. Christ literally dwells in us, abides in us, whenever we take of this Holy bread and drink of this Holy drink. And I guess it is not so supernatural as one might suppose because if you think about it ... where does bread go when you eat it? Or where does wine end up when you drink it? It ends up inside of your body! So, it is true, that when we eat of the bread at communion, which symbolically represents the flesh and body of Christ, we are ingesting it into ourselves, and there it goes down into our bodies, and so abides *in* us. The bread and wine are truly Jesus Christ living there, as food and drink, abiding spiritually within our bodies, as part of our essence. Somehow this spiritualization of matter (the bread and wine) gives those who partake of it, all the more ability to live better. There are many qualities that manifest themselves as Christ within us, abiding with us, into our lives because we take of this special, most significant Communion with him.

So, what does this all mean to us as ordinary people walking around each day trying not to eat until later in the evening? Well, for one, it connects us infinitely as believers, as fellow Christians, in the body of Christ. We all partake and share one holy bread, one holy wine, that symbolizes one Christ that we eat and drink of. Therefore, we are all one body because He lives in each of us by the same Spirit. "Now you are the body of Christ and individually members of it ... If one member suffers, all suffer together; if one member is honored, all rejoice together" (1 Corinthians 12: 27, 26). We are all connected by the pure fact that we believe in the same, one and only true Lord, and celebrate this absolute faith by partaking of one Holy Communion that allows Jesus to abide and dwell in each of us by symbolically eating his flesh (the bread), and drinking his blood (the wine). And it stays and abides in us just as any normal food or drink stays and lives inside us for a time. However, this spiritual kind of bread and wine is very supernatural in essence and gives eternal life, whereas the ordinary food we consume each day does not. Jesus wants us to seek after His flesh, body, life, works, blood, passion, and everything about him before we seek after the ordinary pleasures and common blessings of regular food and drink. That is how critical he is in our survival and way of life. If we have chosen him as our personal Lord and Savior, and claim to be true Christians, then truly, remembering the flesh and blood of Jesus and having Communion with him is in every way more important to our ultimate well being each day than even something as crucial as food and drink. The way we should be seeking and loving and needing him, is with the fervor and intensity we have for food and drink when we are hungry and thirsty because he is our spiritual food and he is our spiritual drink. Then Jesus declared, "I am the bread of life. He who comes to me will never go hungry, and he who believes in me will never be thirsty" (John 6: 35).

Think about how hungry you get throughout the day and the constant thoughts you have about food. That is how often we should be thinking about Jesus and being conscious that his spirit abides in us. Think about how after a long day of fasting, with what excitement, gratitude, and fervor the hands fly to prepare a delicious meal . . . that is the same fervor and passion we should have for Christ and reach to study his Word. Or how, incredibly good that long awaited food is to our bodies—how grateful we are for every healthy bite, and how much we truly love that food (almost more than anything at the moment), that the Father has given us. That is exactly how we should feel about Christ! Fasting helps us to get our priorities straight and better understand the placement of ordinary versus spiritual food in the Bible. One is ordinary and dies within us, while one is extraordinary and causes us to live forever. We need to daily seek after the One that allows us to live forever, and not get stuck on or distracted by the ordinary food that merely serves the appetite.

- *Meditate for 10 minutes*, preferably outside. Enjoy every minute of calm, relaxation without any intrusive thoughts.
- *Pray for 10 minutes.*
- *Enter All Data in Personal DRL.*

JOURNEY JOURNAL

But now in Christ Jesus you who once were far off have been brought near by the blood of Christ. For he himself is our peace, who has made us both one and has broken down in his flesh the dividing wall of hostility.

EPHESIANS 2: 13-14

Write about some of your favorite foods and how you feel when you get to eat them. Is this a momentary or long lasting pleasure? How does knowing that we are saved in Christ provide much more long-lasting, real pleasure rather than a fleeting few minutes of bodily enjoyment? (Go to Sunday's free journal if you need more room)

DAY 30, TUESDAY

Or do you not know that your body is a temple of the Holy Spirit within you, whom you have from God? You are not your own, for you were bought with a price. So glorify God in your body.

1 CORINTHIANS 6: 19-20

We can worship and commune with God anytime, anywhere, not just at church on Sunday morning. One of the greatest blessings I have received from my journey with fasting and meditation is what I am about to share with you now. I hope you will receive and come to fully appreciate it as well. There are two types of Christians: the ones who go to church looking all pretty and do all the right things, and volunteer heavily at all times for the Church but do most things to be seen and approved by other people. They are all about image. They are all about what other people—especially in the social Church hierarchy—think about them "for they loved the glory that comes from man more than the glory that comes from God" (John 12: 43). And they only allow you to see what they want you to see, and are very careful of presenting this great image to the world that may or may not reflect true Christian morals.

Now, the second type of Christian is the one who truly believes all of what it says in the Word of God and strives to live this out in their everyday, personal lives. These I call *everyday Christians*. Integrity was once defined to me as doing what is right when you know nobody else can see you. This is the key to true Christians living for the approval of God alone. It is being faithful and doing good works all the time when no one else knows or can see you. It is God and not for others that you are seeking to please. Simply because you know it is the right thing to do, and *always*—anytime, anywhere strive to do what is right and not what is wrong (sin) in God's eyes. Especially, when no one else is looking, this internal moral integrity shows a deep understanding and adherence to Christ-like values and living. These are all the words, deeds, daily actions, and thoughts we have all the time, everyday, all day long behind closed doors—in the office, in the home, with our children and spouse, by ourselves, doing what we do. Thus, we have the choice constantly a thousand times a day to do the right and honorable thing that brings glory to God even though nobody else may know about it, or do things for the praise and attention of the outside world of people around. Fasting is a powerful spiritual weapon because it connects us every minute, on a second by second basis with the body, and therefore with the body of Christ. It helps make us aware of what we do, think, act, and say every minute of every day because that is how minutely urgent is the necessity and thought of food! We gain a heightened spiritual awareness through this holy practice that aids in bringing awareness to many other aspects of our daily, personal lives and separating what is good for Christ, and how we can improve.

Because our body is the temple that the Holy Spirit dwells within, we are like a mobile church in our very selves! Yes, we still need to go to church, but it is not just merely at church that we can worship and serve God. There are ways to serve and honor the Lord *everyday* in your home, or whatever you do. There are many incredible, spiritual ways that we can integrate into our lives everyday to build them up as fortresses for Christ. Daily meditation, prayer, fasting, giving to the poor, reading the Word of God, listening to uplifting holy music are some of the best ways to be in greater, continual communion with God! These daily spiritual practices show the Father that we love and care about him enough to put as much time as possible into following the Spirit of Truth. By giving up our bodies to such disciplines as fasting, meditation, and daily prayer, we are professing a desire and will to make him central in our personal lives. Truly, it is the way we live that makes us true believers and followers of Christ. And so, by integrating these proven biblical paths into our everyday, personal life we exponentially increase and enhance our relationship with Christ and the Father. Greater endurance in the faith is established. The omniscient light knows all, sees all, penetrates through all darkness, and has created all things. So, let us always do honorable and good things with our bodies and work to serve him at all times, not just when it is convenient or somebody is watching. Let us fast, pray, study the Bible, and meditate today and many more days to grow spiritually as true Christians who live the Word with our actions, not just our talk. May we grow in strength, faith, and abundance as we carry out these humble, yet powerful, providential gifts from the Spirit for how to live better lives in the world.

- *Meditate for 10 minutes*, preferably outside. "I meditate on your precepts and fix my eyes on your ways" (Psalm 119: 15).
- *Pray for 10 minutes.*
- Enter All Data in Personal DRL.

JOURNEY JOURNAL

For His eyes are upon the ways of a man, and he sees all his steps.
JOB 34:21

He provides them with security, and they are supported; and His eyes are on their ways.
JOB 24:23

The eyes of the LORD are in every place, watching the evil and the good.
PROVERBS 15:3

Write some of the different factors that motivate us as people to gain approval from people, and live for the outside world's image of us, versus living every day in our personal, private lives for God and what He would deem as right and so gain his approval? Why is the interior, emotional health in the life of the Christian more important spiritually than the exterior façade many who live for the outer world have?

DAY 31, WEDNESDAY

Do you not know that your bodies are members of Christ?
1 CORINTHIANS 6:15

Treat your body as you would treat the body of Jesus Christ. That is a golden, yet extremely difficult, ideal to follow. Would you pollute the body of the Lord with smoke, excess alcohol, or too much food? Would you force him to do sexually immoral acts of selfish indulgence or dirty up the church body? Whatever we do to ourselves, we, in a way, do to Jesus. "But he who is joined to the Lord becomes one spirit with him" (1 Corinthians 6:17). Because, we are joined to him, we are inseparable from Christ in spirit. Therefore, anything we do to our bodies, affects our spirit, and thus is felt by the Lord. That is why it is of paramount importance that we not sin against our body, but be as honorable as possible in everything we do with it.

Let's talk about the body and what is honorable and brings glory to God who made us. We need to take care of this beautiful temple that he created to bring honor and glory. That means eating healthy, nutritious food and not too much of it. It means exercising often and performing proper hygiene with adequate attention to appearance. It means not taking in harmful chemicals, drugs, or alcohol (in excess). It means not being sexually immoral, but that is out of the scope for today . . . Now, since we are doing a Great Lent fast, I am going to dwell primarily on the importance of eating healthy, nutritious food, and not in excess. Fasting helps us learn to do this in abundance! It is one of the greatest, most perfect blessings for learning to have a well-balanced, nutritious diet that pleases the Lord. There is a reason why fasting was God-ordained as a worshipful activity. Do you think he would have his creation, his own people engaged in something that was not good for them? Do you think Jesus, who knew no sin, would do something for forty days and forty nights that was in someway harmful, bad, or not in line with God's will? No, fasting is a wonderful healthy spiritual activity for the soul that encompasses and facilitates the growth of the mind, body, and spirit all together.

Fasting teaches you how to eat mindfully and with a purpose. No more of this casual, constant snacking or half-planned meals. No more eating just to be eating because it is there. Everything you eat should be carefully recorded in the DRL to cultivate honesty and accountability. Sometimes, we as humans feel that what we do does not matter and that our lives are somehow insignificant and meaningless. Well, the Lord does truly care more than we could ever comprehend about everything we do, and don't do. What we do and say matters and we must believe that or else we will make mistakes, thinking that it does not matter. What you eat and take in to the holy temple matters to Christ because he is joined to it!

As Christians, we need to learn to take care of our bodies as if they were divine structures, given to us with the exact purpose of being tenants of for a while until we go to heaven. They are not only ours, to do with whatever we want, and yet we treat them as such far too often. We should view ourselves as *stewards* of our bodies, entrusted to care for this bodily temple, just as we would attend to Christ, until he returns. That means eating healthy food, and not too much, exercising at least four days a week (or as you are able), and caring for yourself in a positive way. Seems simple right? It is deceptively simple and all too easy because this is an everyday commitment—everyday, for as long as life on earth continues! It's always the same, it never changes, but for some reason seems to be incredibly difficult because look at the destruction of the average American temple walking around.

There is this myth that we need to eat a lot, three meals a day or else we are not fulfilling this idea of what is healthy for our body. We do not need to eat that much food! Especially as we get older. That is why simply having one humble meal in the evening, according to the fasting guidelines, should be enough. Following this rule enables us to achieve balance in our diet and understand truly how much our body needs to function properly (or even better), versus what it just wants or is in a bad habit of consuming. You do not know until you try, right? It may come as a surprise that we do not actually need to eat as much food as we think we do, or have been accustomed to, in order to do everything we need to and want, but this is verily the case. Unless the body is developing, or pregnant and nursing, or very elderly, it does not need as much food as we are accustomed to give it. True, fasting is quite restrictive, and I'm not at all saying we should eat this way all the time, but for forty days it is a valuable experience of learning and understanding more about the body itself and how we can better glorify God in it. Hopefully each one of you will take away copious treasures of how to live better, healthier lives in the way of better eating habits in diet and nutrition. Fasting naturally molds this knowledge into the best possible fit for each individual by disrupting our normal, old eating habits and forging new ones.

- *Meditate for 10 minutes*, preferably outside. "May the arrogant be put to shame for wronging me without cause; but I will *meditate* on your precepts" (Psalm 119: 78).
- *Pray for 10 minutes.*
- *Enter All Data in Personal DRL.*

JOURNEY JOURNAL

For we know that if the tent that is our earthly home is destroyed, we have a building from God, a house not made with hands, eternal in the heavens.

2 CORINTHIANS 5:1

Write some of the most difficult aspects of fasting you have encountered. How have you overcome these challenges to stay with the fast?

CHAPTER 12

WEEK 6—OUR BODY IS THE TEMPLE

KEYS OF LIFE: POWER OF CHANGE

> *This week's reading:* "Fasting is the advocate of repentance. Adam and Eve disobeyed God: they refused to fast from the forbidden fruit. They became slaves of their own desires. But now through fasting, through obedience to the rules of the Church regarding the use of spiritual and material goods, we may return to the life in Paradise, a life of communion with God. Thus, fasting is a means of salvation, this salvation being a life we live in accordance with the Divine will in communion with God.

Because of the liberating effect of fasting, both material and spiritual, the Church has connected fasting with the celebration of the major feasts of our tradition. Easter is, of course, our main feast. It is the "feasts of feasts." It is the feast of our liberation from the bondage of sin, from corrupted nature, from death. For on that day, through His Resurrection from the dead, Christ has raised us "from death to life, and from earth to heaven" (Resurrection Canon), Christ, "our new Passover," has taken us away from the land of slavery, sin and death, to the promised land of freedom, bliss and glory; from our sinful condition to resurrected life.

> It is most appropriate to prepare for this celebration through a liberating fast, both material and spiritual. This is the profound meaning that fasting takes during the Great Lent. Let us allow

ourselves to take advantage of the spiritual riches of the Church. Let us use the precious messianic gifts offered to us through its sacramental life, through its celebrations of the central mysteries of our salvation in Christ."[1]

SUGGESTED AT-HOME ACTIVITY:

Buy one helium balloon from the store with a long string on it. Write down as many prayer requests as you would like on a little piece of paper, roll it up like a scroll, and tie it to the end of the balloon string. Make sure no hardcore environmentalists are watching and release the balloon carrying your prayers up into the heavenly atmosphere! Make sure to smile, or even laugh if you feel like it, as you do it!

---

1. Maximos, "On Fasting," lines 20–33.

DAY 32, THURSDAY

As you come to him, a living stone rejected by men but in the sight of God chosen and precious, you yourselves like living stones are being built up as a spiritual house, to be a holy priesthood, to offer spiritual sacrifices acceptable to God through Jesus Christ.

1 PETER 2: 4-5

Again, we see our very selves, our bodies, being compared to living stones that are part of a holy temple of God. We must keep our bodies as pure as physically possible for this great edifice that the Lord is building. Fasting helps us purify our minds, spirits, and souls from ungodly sin, and it also majorly helps us purify our bodies from impurities such as chemicals found in unhealthy food and drinks. By adhering to a set of guidelines that promote healthy, nutritious food in moderation, we teach ourselves how to become purer vessels for the Lord. In giving up excessive indulgences, or certain types of unhealthy foods, we sacrifice our own pleasure and comfort for the ultimate goal of purifying our bodies into more fit temples for him to dwell. All the unnecessary impurities, fat, and excessive carbohydrates found in most overly processed foods on the market are cleansed from our system as we fast from food altogether, and then, when we do eat, are more mindful about what foods are taken into the bodily temple. The body naturally purifies itself from the excess garbage and common pollution we put into it as nothing solid is consumed all day long, and then what is enjoyed during the evening meal is of much better, nutritious quality. It allows the person to focus on what food actually is and why and when it is being eaten to begin with. It brings vast awareness to the reality of food itself and helps us appreciate it for what it is all anew. Rejuvenation occurs both at the molecular level and in the intellectual processes as believers open up their hearts to this new way of living closer to the Lord. When what is allowed is closer to what God has naturally made: fruit, vegetables, grain, and wholesome seeds and nuts. He did not make the highly processed, unhealthy foods that we need to go without. True God made animals, fish, and eggs too for us to eat, but we are going without those for awhile and focusing on all the rest of the natural abundance the Almighty has created for us to enjoy. Why do we need to make anything else than what God has already made for us to eat? Let us merely combine the gifts of nature (beans, rice, potatoes, corn, apples, anything from seed) and live well. Fasting is a spiritual sacrifice that pleases God. Newness abounds everyday, everywhere as it forces fasters to branch out of their comfort level. For instance, my favorite kind of food is

Indian food. But when I have the opportunity to visit a city during Lent and go to an Indian food restaurant—because we live in the middle of nowhere, literally; in central, rural Wyoming—I have to order the vegetarian dishes. I have expanded my appreciation considerably of the variety and deliciousness of Indian food because I had to; otherwise I never would have! From this, I have grown to love all kinds of vegetarian foods (including veggie sub-sandwiches) I never before knew even existed. Living by a different set of rules for a while teaches us so many incredible things about branching out, trying new things, and exploring other creative ways of doing things and is just one of the hundreds of manifold blessings and gifts this discipline offers!

A diet void of meat, dairy, eggs, alcohol, and other highly processed foods or excess sugar is just simply better for the body (at least for a while). We do not need so much meat or dairy in our diets to get proper protein. There are plenty of ways to get to the same destination—healthier, purer, more vibrant bodies. Beans, nuts, spinach, broccoli, granola, lentils, whole grains, and non-dairy milks are all excellent sources of protein and provide plenty of it for what the bodily actually needs. As fasting purifies our bodies and facilitates the process of refining them into holier temples for the Lord to dwell, we also feel better, naturally, because we are closer to the vine of what God has created. Ever notice how sometimes after a heavy meal at a restaurant of who knows what is actually in it, you just felt almost sick? That awful, yucky sensation that stays in the gut after eating too much, or overly laden, rich food is absent in a nice, long fast. No longer is there an unpleasant, disgusting feeling that lives in our bodies, but instead, a fresh, pure, new essence fills all. Admittedly, hunger does creep in and threaten our resolve, but as long as we pray to Jesus to help us endure and surrender our spirits to him, we can get over those fleeting pangs onto greener banquets of everlasting joy and happiness. We can feel so, so incredibly much better and be emptied of all that yucky, sluggishness of previous bad food and habits; only to be entirely filled by the wonder of peace and revitalized energy of being that comes from dedication to this precious, ancient gift. Once realized it is never looked down upon, but placed on a high, sacred shelf for all time and retrieved anytime or given to someone else in need of complete replenishment.

- *Meditate for 10 minutes*, preferably outside. "My eyes stay open through the watches of the night, that I may meditate on your promises" (Psalm 119:148).
- *Pray for 10 minutes.*
- Enter All Data in Personal DRL.

JOURNEY JOURNAL

For we know that if the tent that is our earthly home is destroyed, we have a building from God, a house not made with hands, eternal in the heavens.

2 COR 5: 1

Write about some of the ways you have had to branch out or get creative with cooking in order to stay within the strict fasting guidelines. Did you end up liking this new way of tasting different foods or cooking more than you thought? Journal about anything as it relates to the new ways you have had to adjust to accommodate to this new way of eating amidst not eating. Go the end of the week, Sunday's Journal for more room if needed.

DAY 33, FRIDAY

Do not conform to the pattern of this world, but be transformed by the renewing of your mind. Then you will be able to test and approve what God's will is—his good, pleasing and perfect will.

ROMANS 12: 2

One of the keys of life that can be discovered and saved for all time during a long fast is the power to change. Few things in life possess the true power to change a person stuck deep in their ruts. We humans get in a habit of doing the same things everyday: eat, work, play, sleep . . . eat, work, play, eat, sleep, etc. That is the nature of the universe. The day repeats itself over and over again with little variation and it is very easy to get stuck in a habit of doing something over and over again. Habits are actions we do on a daily basis, such as eating, taking a walk, sleeping on our side, and kissing our spouse goodbye, etc. Now, it is dangerously easy to get in bad habits on a personal level because we're around these truths everyday. Then, once we begin a bad habit—such as smoking, eating too much or eating the wrong foods, drinking alcohol in excess, or vanity—these habitual, wrong choices land us into deeper and deeper ruts that are hard to get out of. Most often, a great change is necessary to get us people extracted from the terrible ruts we dig as we chug around the yearly calendar. Well, I've got great news! Fasting is a tremendously helpful and effective spiritual tool to causing very true, real, and powerful change.

How does fasting as a divine, ancient gift of the early church enable us to actually change? In its essence, it is the transformative call to a different way of living! Yes, it offers a new way of Christian life that disrupts previous, old patterns and replaces them with better, new ones. It gets rid of those harmful addictions and bad eating habits for at least forty days—as long as you follow the rules—and will change those who do it for the better! At the very least, it will cause Christians to look at food in a new light and hopefully carry many of the spiritual lessons gained into their daily lives. As a discipline, fasting requires us to leave our old, customary habits and ways to enter into a whole new world of trust in the Lord. We have to depend on him instead of the habitual pleasure and filling up on food. There is a certain surrender of the spirit that once we do submit to his will makes life in general goes much easier.

Take someone who eats too much eggs and bacon for breakfast, followed by random snacking throughout the day, including lattes, ice cream, and more heavy food for dinner. Once they dedicate themselves to this forty-day-long fast they are not going to be able to do that anymore and stay honestly within the rules. Therefore, their lifestyle and eating habits *must* change as they enter into a new way of living. Of course, it is very difficult to give up our comfort, pleasure, and material gratifications for the promise of spiritual blessings and greater communion with God, but that is the way it is! For those that truly do commit themselves to fasting as best they can, I promise great, positive changes for the better in their lives. When you apply the power that comes from fasting to various aspects of your daily walk with the Lord, certain old, undesirable habits can finally be extracted forever and replaced with fresh, clean ones. You will grow spiritually in ways you never even knew possible before and your body will feel better than it has for a long, long time. The Word of God will become food for you and more appealing than ever, and fill you with a sustaining grace far surpassing anything else. But after the forty days do we return to our old habits or sinful ways? No, of course not! We hold close and treasure the blessings gained through this new way of living and take it with us for good. We allow ourselves to be transformed and truly changed no matter how hard and uncomfortable that may be. It is possible, and it will happen, as long as you let it happen and surrender to God's graceful power.

- *Meditate for 10 minutes*, preferably outside. "I remember the days of long ago; I meditate on all your works and consider what your hands have done" (Psalm 143:5).
- *Pray for 10 minutes.*
- *Enter All Data in Personal DRL.*

JOURNEY JOURNAL

Put on then as God's chosen ones, holy and beloved, compassionate hearts, kindness, humility, meekness, and patience, bearing with one another and, if one has a complaint against another, forgiving each other; as the Lord has forgiven you, so you also must forgive. And above all these put on love, which binds everything together in perfect harmony.

COLOSSIANS 3:12-14

Journal about some of your habits that you notice have changed as a result of fasting forty days. Describe, as best you can, these changes—perhaps in different areas of your everyday life—and how you feel about them.

DAY 34, SATURDAY

Creative Space Page

Record *any* and *everything* you eat and at what exact time in the DRL. This is never an option. It is always mandatory and one of the 3 cardinal rules.

PALM SUNDAY
Free Day

JOURNEY JOURNAL

Blessed is the one whose transgression is forgiven, whose sin is covered. Blessed is the man against whom the LORD counts no iniquity, and in whose spirit is no deceit.

PSALM 32:1-2

DAY 35, MONDAY

In that day you will know that I am in my Father, and you in me, and I in you. Whoever has my commandments and keeps them, he it is who loves me. And he who loves me will be loved by my Father, and I will love him and manifest myself to him.

JOHN 14:20-22

When you love someone what do you want more than anything on earth? To be near them as much as possible, as close as possible, and as much of the time as possible! This is the way we feel about our children, our best friends, our own parents when we were young, and our husbands or wives (most of the time)! When you love something with your mind, soul, and body, you want to be with it all the time, connected to it through and through, so that there is no beginning or end between you and it, nor is there any second when you cannot stand to be away from the beloved. This is the way Jesus feels about us, and the connection He has with the Father and also desires for us. This is why we cannot limit our love for the Lord to church on Sundays or a few charity projects during the year. We must carry out our love and faith of the Lord every minute of every day to be truly living life with him to the fullest and making the most out of what he has to give us!

As we established last week, since our bodies are the temple of Christ, and as members of the church we are the body of Christ, we can safely stay connected to Jesus all the time, wherever we go. Because we carry him inside of us, just as he carries us with him, the Holy Spirit is with us at all times, every minute of every day, just waiting to be explored, cherished, understood, and made free for the immense power it is. There are a few, God-ordained ways to come into immediate contact with the Holy Spirit and reside more completely in communion with the Lord. The easiest and best spiritual ways to get into closer contact, everyday with Jesus are through meditation, prayer, studying the Word of God, and fasting in your personal, daily life. You can truly do it anytime, anywhere and feel the immediately healing influence of the Lord's peace, love, and new life. By practicing these awesome spiritual ways on an everyday basis we gain immense gifts and weapons to overcome sin, be free, and live firmly in God's grace forever. By disciplining the mind and body for incredible spiritual growth—to sit still at least once a day in meditation and prayer while fasting as well—there is nothing the soul cannot accomplish. The closeness this brings us with Jesus in our ordinary Christian walk with him is unprecedented. We become filled with his incomparable love until we are overflowing with further peace, grace, and countless blessings besides. All we have to do is meditate, fast, and pray regularly to become an *everyday Christian* and connect with Christ on an unbelievably high level rich in faith and understanding of the Word of God.

How often a day—whether we are fasting or not—do we have a thought about food? Or, how many times a day do we have to buy it, make it, or serve it to others in order to make life work? Dozens and dozens of times multiplied! We are constantly having thoughts about food . . . Wondering where we are going to get it, what we are going to make for dinner, or reminded of it as we drive by anything! Now, for the sake of Great Lent, let's capture each of those thoughts about food and turn them into opportunities to think, meditate, or pray with Christ. Take each thought about food and transform it into an opportunity to connect with the spirit inside you which is connected every second of every minute of every day with Christ eternal. That is the kind of transformation I want fasting to bring to each of you. To be filled with a newfound level of personal relationship from abiding that much more fully, every minute, of everyday with Christ. Whenever you are hungry, or have a thought about food, or are cooking it for the kids in the kitchen, turn it into an amazing connection with the Lord, and thereby the Father and experience the journey. Let the constant thoughts of food turned into Christ transform into a newfound awareness and spiritual connection to the Savior and just dwell in the love therein. Know that as you depart from the material consumption of food constantly, yet still have thoughts of it, you can use that moment to moment frequency of thoughts and desires for food and direct them Christward. This constancy of redirecting our thoughts, energy, and focus towards Christ instead of on the immediate gratification of just consuming the food, allows us to exist in an eternal, true present with him spiritually. We are thus more connected every second of every minute in the eternal present to his everlasting love, peace and true joy that much more powerfully. Warning: once it is experienced it is hard to go back!

- *Meditate for 10 minutes*, preferably outside. "Oh, how I love your law! I meditate on it all day long. Your commands are always with me and make me wiser than my enemies. I have more insight than all my teachers, for I meditate on your statutes" (Psalm 119: 97–99).
- *Pray for 10 minutes.*
- *Enter All Data in Personal DRL.*

JOURNEY JOURNAL

Blessed are those who hunger and thirst for righteousness, for they shall be satisfied.

MATTHEW 5:6

Write about what else besides food you find yourselves thinking about like a hundred times a day. Maybe thoughts of your child, your appearance, your phone, what others are doing or thinking, or your significant other consume these? How can you also fast from these other constant distractions to gain closer communion with Christ?

DAY 36, TUESDAY

Isaiah said of the rebellious people who; "Keep on hearing, but do not understand; keep on seeing, but do not perceive." Make the heart of this people dull, and their ears heavy, and blind their eyes; lest they see with their eyes, and hear with their ears, and understand with their hearts, and turn and be healed.

ISAIAH 6: 9-10

What use are eyes that do not see, or ears that do not hear? They are absolutely pointless; like a bike without wheels or a bucket with holes in it. When the things that God designed fail to serve their sole objective they cease to be worth anything. They do become meaningless and unfit—worthless to anybody or anything. Sometimes we as Christians can actually feel like that . . . I know I have, anyways. Feeling like what I do doesn't matter, that it's so insignificant to this great, big, majestic Creator a hundred million miles away in heaven . . . especially when I would compare myself to the rest of the human race and all the spectacular deeds and feats done in the world. I felt that way a lot until I discovered the ancient ways of living a holier life closer to God each day in practicing meditation, prayer, and fasting. I used to want to serve God more all the time but didn't know how, I used to want to do more great things for humanity but had three kids at home, I used to want to be someone important, until I finally realized and could truly *feel* everyday, all day long, for the first time, that I was. By incorporating the amazing rituals of meditation, fasting, and prayer into my daily routine, my life was completely transformed permanently. I could actually feel and know God's love through Jesus for little me and abide in His peace. A kind of spiritual high resulted as I daily walked closer to the Lord as ultimate Joy, Happiness, and eternal Comfort filled my being. I came to understand that I could serve the Lord in meaningful ways in my home, or wherever I was, by integrating these life-saving spiritual practices into my personal routine! And best of all, it does matter.

Besides meditation and prayer, fasting provides a sense of purpose in regards to our eating habits and relationship with food. It gives certain rules and guidelines to live within in order to achieve more discipline, honesty, and self-control. Importantly, it gives us a sense of purpose and meaning to food and eating which is a huge part of life. Therefore, since we have dedicated fasting to the Lord, greater purpose and meaning to our personal lives at large is felt. We live more for him in everyday life and this brings us irreversibly closer in every way. There is greater significance to our thoughts, words, and deeds when their purpose is to honor and serve him. When we do what we are supposed to be doing, in serving God humbly and with integrity, then our purpose is reached. Fasting helps us discover what that sense of purpose is, for each individual person, and to live in it! It gives our lives deeper meaning as our everyday walk with Jesus is strengthened in faith, purpose, trust, and understanding. The relationship between us as his followers, and who he is as the sovereign Lord, is improved vastly in unbelievable ways, which is a mystery uniquely unfolding to each Christian.

You do not have to be a monk to seek to live holier, purer lives serving the Lord everyday. While true monks live set apart in monasteries, what do they do all day? They primarily meditate, fast, pray, and study the Word of God. Now, we can do all that in our own homes too! Picture your home as a sanctuary and your body as the temple of the in-dwelling Spirit of God. You can set aside time and space anytime in the comfort of your own home and be immediately transformed in closer communion with Jesus Christ. It does not take huge trips across the world doing missionary work, or racking your brain on how you can end world hunger . . . it takes setting aside the time for the Lord each day and personally living for him in your heart. Just ten minutes of meditation could grow to twenty, and greater confidence in prayer. Fasting is something you can do around the clock—at home, at work, walking around the neighborhood—and allows you that blessed assurance of constant contact and access to the Spirit he brings. The point is, you don't have to necessarily go anywhere to worship and glorify God because the kingdom of heaven lives inside you, he lives inside you. Meditation, fasting, and prayer, help you access and utilize this immense storehouse of power within you to serve the King of Kings and Lord of Lords in your daily life. By integrating and weaving these holy practices into our ordinary routines we become better, holier vessels ourselves—purer channels of his everlasting grace, justice, and redeeming truth. Our very existence necessarily becomes more worshipfully spiritual, as we serve him more and more as a normal part of our waking hours in private life. This produces greater intimacy in the relationship between us and Jesus and the understanding of God's Word.

Please understand, that I am not stating that fasting, meditation, or prayer are replacements for going to church, participating in Bible studies, and ongoing fellowship with the congregation. They are not. The truest worship always happens in the Church; but meditation, fasting, and prayer are simply spiritual, *worshipful*, ways of honoring and serving God anytime, anywhere, in body, mind, and spirit. They are never replacements or even come close to the holiness and truth of worship in the church with the body of Christ. These modes of serving and honoring God in our bodies should be seen merely as spiritual disciplines and practices, meant for God's glory. Practicing these ancient spiritual ways are not a replacement or substitute for worship with the congregation at church. It is an addition to the foundation, an enhancement to Christian living, and an opportunity for growth in faith and knowledge. Worshipping at church with other believers in the body of Christ is essential and important and irreplaceable.

- *Meditate for 10 minutes*, preferably outside. "Blessed is the man who walks not in the counsel of the wicked, nor stands in the way of sinners, nor sits in the seat of scoffers; but his delight is in the law of the LORD, and on his law he *meditates* day and night" (Psalm 1: 1–3).
- *Pray for 10 minutes.*
- *Enter All Data in Personal DRL.*

JOURNEY JOURNAL

For thus said the Lord God, the Holy One of Israel, "In returning and rest you shall be saved; in quietness and in trust shall be your strength."
ISAIAH 30: 15

Write about anything you would like to below.

DAY 37, WEDNESDAY

He himself bore our sins in his body on the tree, that we might die to sin and live to righteousness. By his wounds you have been healed. For you were straying like sheep, but have now returned to the Shepherd and Overseer of your souls.

1 PETER 2: 24

It is hard for any of us to comprehend the magnitude of the sacrifice that Jesus made in giving his life to suffer brutally on the cross for the forgiveness of our sins. There is no greater love than a person who gives their life, out of love for someone else, in order to save them. It is the quintessential heroic act of all time, throughout all of history. And also think of what the disciples and apostles sacrificed in order to follow Jesus: their possessions, their goods, their lives, their homes, their family, their homeland, everything. Think of that level of sacrifice . . . it is nearly incomprehensible, yet that is what Jesus did for each of us, and that is what he asks of his disciples, those of us who desire earnestly to follow him. It is out of pure love that great sacrifice comes. The greater and more true the love, the greater and more willing the sacrifice. God gave his only Son, the Lamb of God, who knew no sin and was the perfect man, to bear the sin of the world for the redemption of souls. We have hope in eternity, in being resurrected after earthly death into immortality because he suffered so that we could be forgiven in order to be at such peace with the eternal Father. Nobody can hope to go through life without encountering some of the sins and temptations of this world. We are all mortally flawed and need the life-saving grace of forgiveness that is a free gift Jesus gives us by his crucifixion and resurrection to take away these flaws, faults, wrong deeds, and sinfulness.

What can we sacrifice and give up for Jesus? What can we give to him who gives us the promise of life after death and a reason for living each day? True, most of us will agree that God is not asking them to give up everything, literally, as the disciples did in order to follow the Lord, but there are many things that we can give up to become better *common* disciples. We most likely cannot give up, nor should we, our actual homes and leave our children and spouse behind to literally (physically) follow the Lord, but we can give up and sacrifice many hindrances that keep us from following him spiritually. If we truly love him, we will give up and sacrifice as much as we possibly can although it will never come close to what Jesus gave up. Part of what Jesus wants us to give up is our sins, our harmful pleasures, excess, indulgences, and character flaws that keep us from loving him more. Maybe it is a love of money or attachment to material possessions that can turn into idolatry. Maybe it is too much reliance on technology and not enough on the natural world God created. This may seem like an odd sacrifice, but it is a spiritual one that Jesus desires. He wants us to give up our sins, turn from that wrongful way of living, and return back to him. The whole reason Jesus came, fulfilling the will of the Father, was that he should die on the cross to take those sins away. That is why he died in the first place, that is why he came to Earth in the first place—so that we might be at peace and restored sanctity with God through his precious, willing sacrifice of himself. So we must give our sins and defects of self-will up to him, for this is what he came for. He made the greatest sacrifice in giving up his very life for those same sins that are common to all humanity, so the least we can do is sacrifice these dirty, little (or big) secrets to him. All we have to do is humbly ask for Jesus to forgive us and remove these sins and defects from our soul and he faithfully will . . . so long as we truly mean it in the heart, and do not keep returning to the sin. Trust him and he will also give you the power to keep from sinning! They will completely and totally be washed away by his supernatural, miraculous grace, and our spirits become as white as snow! By his divine blood spilled on the cross, the unearthly power of it, are our sins and defects utterly removed to never be remembered again. They actually truly vanish! Disappear like snow that melts in the sun! All you have to do is trust in his power to forgive and actually take each sin away—just a little bit of faith—and . . . Voila! It is gone and you are free from its horrible weight and ugliness henceforward. Thank you a million billion trillion times Jesus! Fasting helps us do this by helping to humble ourselves so that we can become aware of what our sins and defects are in the first place. As we give up food, we give up reliance and attachment on the material, and pull back the spiritual curtain into seeing the rest of what lies in our heart, minds, and spiritual lives. Remember, food is just merely symbolic of the greater, much more important spiritual reality of what lies behind the veil. In giving up food, or making that sacrifice, we can better identify and come to a greater understanding of what else we need to give up and sacrifice to the Lord of all. It helps us peel back the layers of the self and get to the nitty-gritty of what we're made of and what we're doing on all levels so that we can accurately see the self, as in a mirror, for what it is. Fasting aids in bringing this spiritual focus to the surface so that we can grow from it. It also is a formidable spiritual weapon in acquiring the resilience to sin and the ability to overcome temptation. So that once we do give it over to the Lord, the gifts of the Spirit help keep us in his Grace, growing as a well-watered plant, with the power to no longer return or be tempted by that old sinful habit.

- *Meditate for 10 minutes*, preferably outside. "On my bed I remember you; I think of you through the watches of the night" (Psalm 63: 6).
- *Pray for 10 minutes.*
- *Enter All Data in Personal DRL.*

JOURNEY JOURNAL

And by that will we have been sanctified through the offering of the body of Jesus Christ once for all.

HEBREWS 10:10

For the wages of sin is death, but the free gift of God is eternal life in Christ Jesus our Lord.

ROMANS 6:23

For our sake he made him to be sin who knew no sin, so that in him we might become the righteousness of God.

2 CORINTHIANS 5:21

Journal about some of your habits that you notice have changed as a result of fasting forty days. Describe, as best you can, these changes—perhaps in different areas of your everyday life—and how you feel about them.

CHAPTER 13

WEEK 7—SACRIFICIAL LOVE

VIRTUE OF THE WEEK: LOVE

This week's reading: "A growing movement is taking place in the body of Christ. As individuals seek to feed their hunger for God, they've dusted off the ancient spiritual discipline of fasting. This is not a trend or a passing fad, but rather a rediscovery of a powerful way to access God in an intimate and authentic relationship, receive answers to prayers, and gain a fresh touch from our loving Father.

As we look to the Word of God, we see that almost every leader fasted. Prayer and fasting were typical in the Jewish spiritual life, and the people of the Bible knew the power of the practice. When they had great needs or were about to experience a great trial, they often sought God's wisdom and intervention through prayer and fasting . . .

"As pressures of the present-day world increases, today's followers of Jesus Christ are seeking a deeper, more meaningful relationship with their Lord. They want a faith that goes beyond Sunday morning. They want their faith to make a difference in their families, their jobs, their everyday surroundings. They want to experience God in order to live a life that is Christ-centered, significant, and a positive witness to the world.

A growing number of Christians from every denomination have taken notice of the God-ordained discipline of fasting. Whether their fasts are corporate or personal, Christians are once again making this ancient practice a normal part of their spiritual routines."[1]

SUGGESTED AT-HOME ACTIVITY:

Choose three of God's attributes (back on p. 21) you feel most inspired by and write them down on a small piece of paper. Put the paper in your purse or wallet—something you carry with you everyday—so that you can remember he is with you always and meditate on his richness wherever you may be. Whenever a moment of need arises or fear or doubt creep in, pull out that piece of paper and dwell spiritually with him in immediate, close communion, as you meditate on each quality.

1. Gregory, *Daniel Fast*, 9, 11.

DAY 38, MAUNDY THURSDAY

I humble myself by fasting, and people insult me; I dress myself in clothes of mourning, and they laugh at me. They talk about me in the streets, and drunkards make up songs about me.

PSALM 69:10-12

Maundy Thursday commemorates the ceremonial washing of the feet of the poor, demonstrated by Jesus when he washed the feet of his disciples. In this ultimate act of humility he teaches us how to be humble and how this prepares us for his death on the cross. Wouldn't it be hard to let the Messiah, the King of all kings, stoop down and wash *your* feet? Can you imagine? It would be so humiliating, so humbling, and this is just what Peter protested when he said; "You shall never wash my feet." But Jesus responded; "If I do not wash you, you have no share with me" (John 13: 8). Christ did this ceremonial washing to show us that we must allow him to serve us, because this is what he came to do: die on the cross so that he could serve us sinners in taking our sins away by God's power. Imagine how helpless you would have to be not to be able to wash your own feet but have to have someone else wash them for you . . . imagine if that someone were Christ and how humiliated you would be for him—the God of all—to come up to you in your humbled state of hopelessness and have to wash them for you. It is this state of hopelessness and helplessness that is the human condition that he came to save us from. Jesus washed the disciples feet in an act that mirrored the sin he would wash away from humanity on the cross shortly to come. However, he does this humiliating act to show us that we, as sinners, just as Peter was, must humble ourselves in order to let him do this great cleansing. Therefore, we have to admit our hopeless, helpless condition in absolute humility. Allow him to "wash our feet," and take away our sin. We must sit down and be truly repentant and sorry for our sin, for our weakness, for our human condition, and let him come and serve us: he who is greater than all. Pride cannot stand in the way or the ego or the conscience or anything that would hinder this sacred act of cleansing forgiveness. Jesus came as a servant, in obedience to the point of death; to serve you and I so that our sins could be forgiven by his precious blood. The least we can do is be humble and repentant, and let him do his will in this.

But being humble and repentant is so hard sometimes, isn't it? It takes both humility and true contrition for personal wrongdoing! Ugh! It is as hard as having to sit there and let Jesus wash your feet! Another ugh!

How can we possibly become humble enough to allow Jesus to serve us in these humiliating ways of washing feet and dying for *us*? It is just so hard to accept that anyone could do that for us, let alone the Lord of all. Such self-sacrificing love is almost incomprehensible, and yet it is so real. Well, fasting is a wonderful way to help humble the self to aid in admitting the helplessness, the hopelessness, and weakness of the human condition. Going without food touches on the basic needs of the human body similar to the washing of the feet to stay clean. It brings us to a place of surrender, of complete spiritual willingness to sit there and let Jesus serve us, in washing away our sins or our feet. In humility, we show by fasting and repentance how much we direly need Jesus to lovingly serve us in what he does, and that we cannot live without him. More important than food is this need and hunger to be saved and loved by him alone. Fasting takes us away from the material and more into the spiritual that helps us become aware of what our sins and faults are, so that we can be truly repentant. Then, once we, as sinners, are repentant and truly sorry about these things we can humbly come before him and pray that he removes these from us in life-saving forgiveness. However, we must be absolutely humble and repentant as we earnestly ask this of him in prayer. It might help to kneel down as a further sign of humility, or lie prostrate on the floor as a sign of helplessness and surrender as we implore the Savior to take away our sin. As long as we humbly allow him to serve us, and truly forgive us, he always, always, faithfully will! By the power of God he reaches into our innermost being and actually, totally removes those filthy sins forever. Voila! Suddenly, they are mystically gone from us from that point forward! No matter how deep the stain of your sins, Jesus removes your sins by his precious blood. Alleluia! Praise be to God!

- *Meditate for 10 minutes*, preferably outside. "Tremble and do not sin; when you are on your beds, search your hearts and be silent" (Psalm 4:4).
- *Pray for 10 minutes.*
- *Enter All Data in Personal DRL.*

JOURNEY JOURNAL

"Come now, let us reason together, says the LORD: though your sins are like scarlet, they shall be as white as snow; though they are red like crimson, they shall become like wool. . ."

ISAIAH 1:18

Describe two different times when you have felt completely helpless, hopeless, or weak. How can we call upon Jesus' life-saving grace of compassion and forgiveness to help us out of such times?

DAY 39, GOOD FRIDAY

Mary therefore took a pound of expensive ointment made from pure nard, and anointed the feet of Jesus and wiped his feet with her hair. The house was filled with the fragrance of the perfume.

JOHN 12: 3

Nard was an extremely precious, costly substance in this time; what Mary did in sacrificing this gift to anoint the feet of her Savior was basically to give all she had. The cost of this much nard would be around $20,000 in today's currency. That is how much she wanted to show her love for Jesus before he was taken to die on the cross for the sins of the world. What do we have to give him? What can we possibly give the King of all the earth who cares not for material things or the old way of sacrifices in bulls, rams, or burnt offerings? He wants us! Our hearts, mind, body, and spirit directed in serving him in righteousness, free from sin. "I appeal to you therefore, brothers, by the mercies of God, to present your bodies as a living sacrifice, holy and acceptable to God, which is your spiritual worship" (Romans 12: 1). By fasting, we present our bodies as instruments for God's grace, for the Spirit to work in and through us, by giving up and sacrificing our comforts and pleasures for his sake. We sacrifice our bodies to hunger, we give our time in learning and exploring how to do so, and we invest our faith as Christians and followers of Christ to become stronger along this Way. It is something we can give to him, something we can sacrifice out of his Divine love. We do not have to go without food, we have *chosen* not to. In this choice, there is a uniting of the self-will; the freedom of choice and free will with the will of God; and in so doing we do what we believe serves his purposes.

Jesus did not *have* to die on the cross. God did not make him do it. He *chose* to—laying down his own self-will and uniting it with the will of his Father. "For this reason the Father loves me, because I lay down my life that I may take it up again. No one takes it from me, but I lay it down of my own accord. I have authority to lay it down, and I have authority to take it up again" (John 10: 17–18). There is no greater love than Jesus sacrificing himself to death for the sake of others. The Lamb of God gave his blood to wash away our sins in the ultimate sacrifice to bring us peace with the Father. "Without the shedding of blood there is no forgiveness" (Hebrews 9: 22) Similar to the old Passover where the blood of lambs were commanded by the Holy Spirit to be put above the doorway so that those living inside would not be put to death; the New Passover, is the blood of the Lamb of

God, who sacrificed himself so that we could live without sin and therefore not die, like those without the blood above their doorway. The blood of the Lamb is on our "doorways," meaning on our hearts, in our minds, and present in the everyday way we live so that death may pass us over, and we be reunited with him in the Kingdom of Heaven. "For the love of Christ controls us, because we have concluded this: that one has died for all, therefore all have died; and he died for all, that those who live might no longer live for themselves but for him who for their sake died and was raised" (2 Corinthians 5: 14–15). So, let us live each day with and for Jesus by giving of ourselves—our time, our comforts and pleasures—while doing so all out of love. Picking up our cross each day and following Him in fasting, meditation, and prayer are ways we can serve in holiness. In divine love, trust, and dependence on him alone, can we come into evermore present, conscious contact with God and grow exponentially as Christians in faith. These ways strengthen the individual Spirit to connect with the Holy Spirit and worship the Father everyday in our personal life, in everything we do, and in the choices we *choose* to unite our will with that above. Finally, our lives are a result of this walk of faith and become better in every way imaginable. Go in peace—serve the Lord!

- *Meditate for 10 minutes*, preferably outside. "Finally, brothers and sisters, whatever is true, whatever is noble, whatever is right, whatever is pure, whatever is lovely, whatever is admirable—if anything is excellent or praiseworthy—think about such things" (Philippians 4: 8).
- *Pray for 10 minutes.*
- *Enter All Data in Personal DRL.*

JOURNEY JOURNAL

A new commandment I give to you, that you love one another: just as I have loved you, you also are to love one another. By this all people will know that you are my disciples, if you have love for one another.

JOHN 13: 34-35

Journal about some of the best presents you have ever given to someone. How does giving our time, our pleasures, our comforts, or bad habits, and indulgences over to Jesus compare to these great gifts of the past? What is easier to give—a store bought, gift-wrapped present or the latter spiritual one? Why?

DAY 40, SATURDAY

Hurray! Last Day! You did it!

Creative Space Page

Record *any* and *everything* you eat, *(for the last time)*, and at what exact time in the DRL. This is never an option. It is always mandatory and one of the 3 cardinal rules.

EASTER SUNDAY!

Celebrate, Christ Is Risen!
He Is Risen Indeed! Alleluia!

Feast Day!

But the angel said to the women, "Do not be afraid, for I know that you seek Jesus who was crucified. He is not here, for he has risen, as he said. Come, see the place where he lay. Then go quickly and tell his disciples that he has risen from the dead, and behold, he is going before you to Galilee; there you will see him. See, I have told you."

MATTHEW 28: 5-7

IN CONCLUSION:

Now, I would encourage you to reflect on how this journey has changed your life, as it has mine, over and over again. And what a miraculous adventure it is, living with the risen Lord, eh? There is nothing that compares to the breathless heights he takes us to, or the depths of love, joy, and faith. It is my hope for each of you, my friends, who have been with me, in our mutual love of the Lord and faith, that you take away a great many lessons from this experience. Lessons that you can apply daily to your lives to always enrich and make them better, for all time. I hope that your personal relationship with Jesus has deepened incredibly more, and will continue to strengthen and grow upwards the rest of the days of your life. In the Journey Journal at the very end, record some of the most important, most valuable lessons that you have learned that you wish to take away. How do you feel, think, and respond to situations (or life perhaps) differently than you did before and what do you want to hold onto more than anything, forever, never to lose? These pearls of wisdom and knowledge, that you have gained, should be written down so that you can look back and reflect on them anytime you have need, for the rest of your days. Don't let them go, don't forget, but remember them in your heart of hearts, and mind, vouchsafed with an eternal lock and key. Consider this illustrious depiction of meditation in Psalms and take that with you as well, along with these lessons and instructions, to remember and reflect back on and *meditate* on anytime: "I remember the days of old; I meditate on all that you have done; I ponder the work of your hands. I stretch out my hands to you; my soul thirsts for you like a parched land" (Psalm 14: 5-6). Remember and utilize all you have gained in spiritual gifts and blessings to continue to grow closer to the Lord and lead great lives!

I will share with you some of the ways fasting for Christ has changed my life . . . with all the immense *discipline* that it invariably creates, I have become much, much better as a parent at disciplining and enforcing rules with my three boys. With the increase in discipline by practicing this ancient way, I have been blessed with spiritual groves of discipline and the ability to instruct, correct, and enforce the right ways amongst my children. I am much more on top of their moment to moment, everyday errors and little wrongdoings, and much more able to recognize these for what they are and properly correct (and punish if necessary) them immediately. As a mother, I feel much more in control of my three boys and the virtuous outcome of the way I am raising them on a daily basis. Much of the virtues that have increased for me personally are those of self-control, temperance, gratitude, and discipline. These virtues gained have helped me in nearly every way of my personal life, and I am just filled with awe and wonder at the manifestation of the Holy Spirit.

As far as self-control and temperance, I find that I am far less wasteful of food, as well as other material things and am in complete control of my monetary spending. No longer do I have unknown charges coming through on my bank account, nor have a need for excessive indulgent purchases that dissolve into nothingness, nor have unnecessary impulse buying whatsoever. Truly, it has been a semi-miraculous change in that regard that the virtues of gaining more self-control and temperance from fasting for Christ, directly cross over into the financial arena for me. It's like the more I have learned to go without food, the more I can easily go without many other material things that I used to think I could not go without! I am able to save so much more money simply because I am truly content in faith and happy in my life; I know fasting has drastically aided in this enlightening process. Material desires have almost ceased to tempt me . . . which is an entirely new sensation for me because I used to want a better this, or a new that, or a nicer whatever . . . like almost every American out there . . . but somehow that has changed! No longer do I dream of a bigger house, cooler car, or nicer flowers. I can truly say I am grateful and content for what I have and the spiritual gifts and blessings the Lord has given me, and the incredible life he has given me, so as to not want a great many more material things. I hope this doesn't sound like I'm settling for mediocrity because I'm not. I just find myself spiritually and emotionally complete in the Lord more and more and this happens to be a far, far better more real and true state of being than anything money can buy. Truly, it pales in comparison after what I have experienced with the Savior so as to leave nothing else desired. "But godliness with contentment is great gain" (1 Timothy 6: 6).

Along the same lines, with greater self-control and temperance and discipline gained through fasting, I have found an amazingly newfound ability to control my temper and listen more than I talk. I have become so much better at just keeping my mouth shut, instead of talking nervously to people I may not know that well, which was something I struggled with before. Now, for the first time, I am so at peace and comfortable with myself that I can just listen as never before and simply be—anywhere, anytime, with anyone! One more instruction for you before I let you go: go back and carefully rip out the list of Innocent pleasures on page 71 to keep. Refer back to it if you're unsure what to do, feeling down, or in doubt. Remember he is always with you and these blessings and gifts are enduring in quality! There are so, so many gifts that I have received from this irreplaceably valuable practice, that I could go on for another two-hundred pages but that would not be the point. The point is for you to take all these treasures with you, now and forevermore, in Christ the Lord. Be closer to him always, and know that you can find him anytime, anywhere, any day—inside yourself—the true Kingdom of Heaven. Eat the true bread, and live in peace, love, and joy always! May our Father in heaven bless you and keep you in his grace and mercy, all the days of your life. Go with God, my friends. The Lord Be with you.

Write down any concluding thoughts, lessons learned, and spiritual gifts gained that you would like to remember for always. Describe, in as much detail as possible, how you feel differently from before the first day of the fast. In what ways have you grown in the virtues and what positive changes have you been able to make as a result? Free write anything and everything else that seems important to your journey, and know that you will always have it to come back to for reflection. "Trust in him at all times, O people; pour out your heart before him; God is a refuge for us" (Psalm 62: 5–8).

JOURNEY JOURNAL

For God alone, O my soul, wait in silence, for my hope is from him. He only is my rock and my salvation, my fortress; I shall not be shaken. On God rests my salvation and my glory; my mighty rock, my refuge is in God.

PSALM 62:5–7

PREPARATION FOR GROUP BIBLE STUDY LENTEN MEAL SWAPS FOR SPIRITUAL LEADERS AND PARTICIPANTS

Have everyone bring a dish, or one full meal, that fits within the strict Christian fasting guidelines to each Group Bible study session. After preparing the meal, make a card to go with it including the name of the dish on one side and the main ingredients and what it consists of on the back of the card. When participants come in for the Bible study, set out all the dishes in a row on a table somewhere in the room with each of the name cards beside each dish to identify it. Then, have everyone sit down for the Bible study and begin.

When it is time for the Lenten meal swap portion of the study, have everyone go around and tell the name of their dish, and a short story as to why it is one of their favorites, or why they brought it to share with others. Share how you chose the ingredients or did certain combinations to fit within the strict fasting rule guidelines. While people are sharing their stories about their Lenten dish, pass around a basket with numbers and have everyone draw a number. From this point, it works just like a white elephant party! Starting with whomever chose number one, they get to go choose whatever dish they want from the banquet table. Then number two goes, and then number three, on down the line until everyone has a new dish to take home that someone else has prepared.

In preparing food for the meal swap please make sure all food is packaged in disposable bags or containers that you do not expect to get back. Do not use any nice plates, bowls, or serving platters. Restrict packaging to large zip-lock bags, recycled yoghurt containers, jars, or Tupperware containers that you do not need returned. The reason for this is simple . . . because we are fasting some of the people may choose not to eat the meal they received at the Bible study that week, but freeze it for another time entirely. Or maybe they do not want to feel pressured to eat that exact meal by any set time which having to give the containers back would invariably cause. That is why when you prepare for the meal swap use only containers you do not care about getting back.

Make sure to relay in your story how you prepared the meal, the special choices of what went into it, and how this might be different from how you would normally cook. The most important ingredient to any and all this is to have fun. Please, please for the love of God have fun!

Group Session Guide #1 (opt.)
CHAPTER 7

WEEK 1—INTO THE WILDERNESS

VIRTUE OF THE WEEK: GRATITUDE

Meet one Day a week for one-hour-and-fifteen minutes once the Fast commences. I recommend Wednesday evenings or Sunday late afternoons, but this is just a suggestion. Meeting as a group is purely optional; this Bible study is created for the individual to do on their own as well.

1. [10 minutes]: Begin with 10 minutes of Guided Meditation to quiet the mind and center the focus on God.

2. [15 minutes]: Refer back to the first page of chapter 1 for the week's *Suggested Reading* and read aloud, or select your own reading from quality Fasting Literature or highly related scripture in the Bible. Afterwards, allow for any comments or questions that arise and have a big group discussion on the topic.

3. [25 minutes]: Conduct the Lenten Meal Swap . . . Refer to the instructions given under *Preparation for Group Bible Study for Spiritual Leaders and Participants* for how to conduct this portion smoothly. Remind people that they are not forced to eat anything; that they are welcome to give their dish away to someone else or freeze for another time. That is why no one should expect any containers back. After all, we *are* fasting!

4. [15 minutes]: Break participants up into pairs or small groups of three to four people, (depending on how many people there are), and have them share their Personal Daily Record Logs with each other. Tell

them that they are welcome to exchange their Logs with each other or keep them to themselves if they feel more comfortable doing that. This is a wonderful time of fellowship, kinship, and motivation in the fasting journey. It also helps keep us accountable for what we truly did and did not do during the week. Encourage them to be open and respectful with each other; sharing the delight of the week with its various ups and downs. Reiterate that there should be no shaming or competition of who ate more or who ate less, but a time of honest sharing to the building up of one another.

5. [10 minutes]: *Prayers of Intercession*: Ask if someone would be willing to close the prayer. Open in prayer with your requests and remembrances, and then say; "and we raise up now any other prayers said aloud or in our hearts," and allow the next person to voice their prayers to the Lord, and then after they have said their prayer, allow for the next person to chime in with their prayer requests, so on and so forth until it is time to close and then either have someone preselected to close the prayer, or do it yourself as the leader.

Group Session Guide #2

CHAPTER 8

WEEK 2—MIND OVER MATTER, SPIRIT OVER FLESH

VIRTUE OF THE WEEK: PATIENCE

1. [10 minutes]: Begin with 10 minutes of Guided Meditation to quiet the mind and center the focus on God.

2. [15 minutes]: Refer back to the first page of chapter 8 for the week's *Suggested Reading* and read aloud, or select your own reading from quality Fasting Literature or highly related scripture in the Bible. Afterwards, allow for any comments or questions that arise and have a big group discussion on the topic.

3. [25 minutes]: Conduct the Lenten Meal Swap . . . Refer to the instructions given under *Preparation for Group Bible Study for Spiritual Leaders and Participants* for how to conduct this portion smoothly. Remind people that they are not forced to eat anything; that they are welcome to give their dish away to someone else or freeze for another time. That is why no one should expect any containers back. After all, we *are* fasting!

4. [15 minutes]: Break participants up into pairs or small groups of three to four people, (depending on how many people there are), and have them share their Personal Daily Record Logs with each other. Tell them that they are welcome to exchange their Logs with each other or keep them to themselves if they feel more comfortable doing that. This

is a wonderful time of fellowship, kinship, and motivation in the fasting journey. It also helps keep us accountable for what we truly did and did not do during the week. Encourage them to be open and respectful with each other; sharing the delight of the week with its various ups and downs. Reiterate that there should be no shaming or competition of who ate more or who ate less, but a time of honest sharing to the building up of one another.

5. [10 minutes]: *Prayers of Intercession*: Ask if someone would be willing to close the prayer. Open in prayer with your requests and remembrances, and then say; "and we raise up now any other prayers said aloud or in our hearts," and allow the next person to voice their prayers to the Lord, and then after they have said their prayer, allow for the next person to chime in with their prayer requests, so on and so forth until it is time to close and then either have someone preselected to close the prayer, or do it yourself as the leader.

SUGGESTED AT-HOME ACTIVITY FOR THIS WEEK:

Get a hammer and 2 nails. Take them outside and find a tree somewhere convenient. Write down your 3 temptations or sins of the world on a piece of paper as well as your 5 personality characteristics of self-will. Nail it to the tree and leave it there for one week. . . until next Wednesday. . . somewhere nobody will see it*!*

Group Session Guide #3

CHAPTER 9

WEEK 3—HEART V. STOMACH

VIRTUE OF THE WEEK: DISCIPLINE

1. [10 minutes]: Begin with 10 minutes of Guided Meditation to quiet the mind and center the focus on God.

2. [15 minutes]: Refer back to the first page of chapter 9 for the week's *Suggested Reading* and read aloud, or select your own reading from quality Fasting Literature or highly related scripture in the Bible. Afterwards, allow for any comments or questions that arise and have a big group discussion on the topic.

3. [25 minutes]: Conduct the Lenten Meal Swap . . . Refer to the instructions given under *Preparation for Group Bible Study for Spiritual Leaders and Participants* for how to conduct this portion smoothly. Remind people that they are not forced to eat anything; that they are welcome to give their dish away to someone else or freeze for another time. That is why no one should expect any containers back. After all, we *are* fasting!

4. [15 minutes]: Break participants up into pairs or small groups of three to four people, (depending on how many people there are), and have them share their Personal Daily Record Logs with each other. Tell them that they are welcome to exchange their Logs with each other or keep them to themselves if they feel more comfortable doing that. This is a wonderful time of fellowship, kinship, and motivation in the fasting journey. It also helps keep us accountable for what we truly did and

did not do during the week. Encourage them to be open and respectful with each other; sharing the delight of the week with its various ups and downs. Reiterate that there should be no shaming or competition of who ate more or who ate less, but a time of honest sharing to the building up of one another.

5. [10 minutes]: *Prayers of Intercession*: Ask if someone would be willing to close the prayer. Open in prayer with your requests and remembrances, and then say; "and we raise up now any other prayers said aloud or in our hearts," and allow the next person to voice their prayers to the Lord, and then after they have said their prayer, allow for the next person to chime in with their prayer requests, so on and so forth until it is time to close and then either have someone preselected to close the prayer, or do it yourself as the leader.

SUGGESTED AT-HOME ACTIVITY FOR THIS WEEK:

Go out and remove the list nailed to your tree of choice and pick somewhere discreet to tear it up into little, tiny pieces. (Don't litter though, that's illegal, and I won't be blamed for leading you into sin). Once that is finished, once again write down your list of 3 sins and/or temptations on a little piece of paper along with your 7 personality characteristics of self-will. Now, find a little box of some kind, put the list in there, and hide the box somewhere nobody will ever find! We are going to leave it there for the next 2 weeks and then it is going to get really exciting what we do next! (Don't read ahead. . .. I know what you're thinking!)

Group Session Guide #4

CHAPTER 10

WEEK 4—THE NUMBER FORTY

VIRTUE OF THE WEEK: PURITY

1. [10 minutes]: Begin with 10 minutes of Guided Meditation to quiet the mind and center the focus on God.

2. [15 minutes]: Refer back to the first page of chapter 10 for the week's *Suggested Reading* and read aloud, or select your own reading from quality Fasting Literature or highly related scripture in the Bible. Afterwards, allow for any comments or questions that arise and have a big group discussion on the topic.

3. [25 minutes]: Conduct the Lenten Meal Swap . . . Refer to the instructions given under *Preparation for Group Bible Study for Spiritual Leaders and Participants* for how to conduct this portion smoothly. Remind people that they are not forced to eat anything; that they are welcome to give their dish away to someone else or freeze for another time. That is why no one should expect any containers back. After all, we *are* fasting!

4. [15 minutes]: Break participants up into pairs or small groups of three to four people, (depending on how many people there are), and have them share their Personal Daily Record Logs with each other. Tell them that they are welcome to exchange their Logs with each other or keep them to themselves if they feel more comfortable doing that. This is a wonderful time of fellowship, kinship, and motivation in the fasting journey. It also helps keep us accountable for what we truly did and

did not do during the week. Encourage them to be open and respectful with each other; sharing the delight of the week with its various ups and downs. Reiterate that there should be no shaming or competition of who ate more or who ate less, but a time of honest sharing to the building up of one another.

5. [10 minutes]: *Prayers of Intercession*: Ask if someone would be willing to close the prayer. Open in prayer with your requests and remembrances, and then say; "and we raise up now any other prayers said aloud or in our hearts," and allow the next person to voice their prayers to the Lord, and then after they have said their prayer, allow for the next person to chime in with their prayer requests, so on and so forth until it is time to close and then either have someone preselected to close the prayer, or do it yourself as the leader.

SUGGESTED AT-HOME ACTIVITY FOR THIS WEEK:

Pick out two different objects, such as pennies, grains of rice, or whatever you can find that is small and count it out to forty. Count it in a line with one object—like a long train with forty carts—and then form it into a pile with the other object. All the while let your mind meditate on the number forty and its significance to you during this fast. Then, once you have forty objects counted out choose a vessel to put them into. Contemplate how you are a like that vessel, containing the spirit of fasting for forty days, and how great it is!

Group Session Guide #5

CHAPTER 11

WEEK 5—SYMBOLIC NATURE OF FOOD

VIRTUES OF THE WEEK: TEMPERANCE & MODERATION

1. [10 minutes]: Begin with 10 minutes of Guided Meditation to quiet the mind and center the focus on God.

2. [15 minutes]: Refer back to the first page of chapter 11 for the week's *Suggested Reading* and read aloud, or select your own reading from quality Fasting Literature or highly related scripture in the Bible. Afterwards, allow for any comments or questions that arise and have a big group discussion on the topic.

3. [25 minutes]: Conduct the Lenten Meal Swap . . . Refer to the instructions given under *Preparation for Group Bible Study for Spiritual Leaders and Participants* for how to conduct this portion smoothly. Remind people that they are not forced to eat anything; that they are welcome to give their dish away to someone else or freeze for another time. That is why no one should expect any containers back. After all, we *are* fasting!

4. [15 minutes]: Break participants up into pairs or small groups of three to four people, (depending on how many people there are), and have them share their Personal Daily Record Logs with each other. Tell them that they are welcome to exchange their Logs with each other or keep them to themselves if they feel more comfortable doing that. This is a wonderful time of fellowship, kinship, and motivation in the fasting journey. It also helps keep us accountable for what we truly did and

did not do during the week. Encourage them to be open and respectful with each other; sharing the delight of the week with its various ups and downs. Reiterate that there should be no shaming or competition of who ate more or who ate less, but a time of honest sharing to the building up of one another.

5. [10 minutes]: *Prayers of Intercession*: Ask if someone would be willing to close the prayer. Open in prayer with your requests and remembrances, and then say; "and we raise up now any other prayers said aloud or in our hearts," and allow the next person to voice their prayers to the Lord, and then after they have said their prayer, allow for the next person to chime in with their prayer requests, so on and so forth until it is time to close and then either have someone preselected to close the prayer, or do it yourself as the leader.

SUGGESTED AT-HOME ACTIVITY THIS WEEK:

Go retrieve your hidden box from wherever it is, with the ominous piece of paper inside... There are a number of ways to perform the following ceremony: you can come quietly to church by yourself sometime with your little box in hand. Sit quietly before the altar in the sanctuary and when you are ready, bring forth your box and set it on the altar before His majesty as you literally give your sins over to Jesus in humble repentance. Another way to do this ceremony is to have the person who usually leads bible study perform the act of taking each of your boxes and placing them on the altar to be given over to the Lord in humble repentance.

Group Session Guide #6

CHAPTER 12

WEEK 6—OUR BODY IS THE TEMPLE

KEYS OF LIFE: POWER TO CHANGE

1. [10 minutes]: Begin with 10 minutes of Guided Meditation to quiet the mind and center the focus on God.

2. [15 minutes]: Refer back to the first page of chapter 12 for the week's *Suggested Reading* and read aloud, or select your own reading from quality Fasting Literature or highly related scripture in the Bible. Afterwards, allow for any comments or questions that arise and have a big group discussion on the topic.

3. [25 minutes]: Conduct the Lenten Meal Swap . . . Refer to the instructions given under *Preparation for Group Bible Study for Spiritual Leaders and Participants* for how to conduct this portion smoothly. Remind people that they are not forced to eat anything; that they are welcome to give their dish away to someone else or freeze for another time. That is why no one should expect any containers back. After all, we *are* fasting!

4. [15 minutes]: Break participants up into pairs or small groups of three to four people, (depending on how many people there are), and have them share their Personal Daily Record Logs with each other. Tell them that they are welcome to exchange their Logs with each other or keep them to themselves if they feel more comfortable doing that. This is a wonderful time of fellowship, kinship, and motivation in the fasting journey. It also helps keep us accountable for what we truly did and

did not do during the week. Encourage them to be open and respectful with each other; sharing the delight of the week with its various ups and downs. Reiterate that there should be no shaming or competition of who ate more or who ate less, but a time of honest sharing to the building up of one another.

5. [10 minutes]: *Prayers of Intercession*: Ask if someone would be willing to close the prayer. Open in prayer with your requests and remembrances, and then say; "and we raise up now any other prayers said aloud or in our hearts," and allow the next person to voice their prayers to the Lord, and then after they have said their prayer, allow for the next person to chime in with their prayer requests, so on and so forth until it is time to close and then either have someone preselected to close the prayer, or do it yourself as the leader.

SUGGESTED AT-HOME ACTIVITY:

Buy one helium balloon from the store with a long string on it. Write down as many prayer requests as you would like on a little piece of paper, roll it up like a scroll, and tie it to the end of the balloon string. Make sure no hardcore environmentalists are watching and release the balloon carrying your prayers up into the heavenly atmosphere! Make sure to smile, or even laugh if you feel like it, as you do it!

Group Session Guide #7

CHAPTER 13

WEEK 7—SACRIFICIAL LOVE

VIRTUE OF THE WEEK: LOVE

1. [10 minutes]: Begin with 10 minutes of Guided Meditation to quiet the mind and center the focus on God.

2. [15 minutes]: Refer back to the first page of chapter 13 for the week's *Suggested Reading* and read aloud, or select your own reading from quality Fasting Literature or highly related scripture in the Bible. Afterwards, allow for any comments or questions that arise and have a big group discussion on the topic.

3. [25 minutes]: Conduct the Lenten Meal Swap . . . Refer to the instructions given under *Preparation for Group Bible Study for Spiritual Leaders and Participants* for how to conduct this portion smoothly. Remind people that they are not forced to eat anything; that they are welcome to give their dish away to someone else or freeze for another time. That is why no one should expect any containers back. After all, we *are* fasting!

4. [15 minutes]: Break participants up into pairs or small groups of three to four people, (depending on how many people there are), and have them share their Personal Daily Record Logs with each other. Tell them that they are welcome to exchange their Logs with each other or

keep them to themselves if they feel more comfortable doing that. This is a wonderful time of fellowship, kinship, and motivation in the fasting journey. It also helps keep us accountable for what we truly did and did not do during the week. Encourage them to be open and respectful with each other; sharing the delight of the week with its various ups and downs. Reiterate that there should be no shaming or competition of who ate more or who ate less, but a time of honest sharing to the building up of one another.

5. [10 minutes]: *Prayers of Intercession*: Ask if someone would be willing to close the prayer. Open in prayer with your requests and remembrances, and then say; "and we raise up now any other prayers said aloud or in our hearts," and allow the next person to voice their prayers to the Lord, and then after they have said their prayer, allow for the next person to chime in with their prayer requests, so on and so forth until it is time to close and then either have someone preselected to close the prayer, or do it yourself as the leader.

SUGGESTED AT-HOME ACTIVITY:

Choose three of God's attributes (back on p. 71) you feel most inspired by and write them down on a small piece of paper. Put the paper in your purse or wallet—something you carry with you everyday—so that you can remember he is with you always and meditate on His richness wherever you may be. Whenever a moment of need arises or fear or doubt creep in, pull out that piece of paper and dwell spiritually with him in immediate, close communion, as you meditate on each quality.

CHAPTER 14

RECIPE COLLECTION

"Give us this Day Our Daily Bread"

BASIL-CILANTRO PESTO

- 1 big bunch Cilantro
- ¾ C. Nut Blend
- 1 Cup Water (more if needed for paste)
- ¼ tsp. salt
- ¾ C. fresh Basil leaves

- 1/8 tsp. crushed red pepper
- 1 clove garlic
- ¼ tsp. black pepper
- 2 T. Olive oil
- ¼ tsp. ground white pepper

To Make: Put all ingredients into a food processor (or blender). Add water until thick paste forms. Add more water if necessary. You want it to be as thick as possible without being runny, yet still spreadable. Make more as needed for later recipes—double the recipe now if desired to save time. Store in appropriate size Tupperware container, or reusable plastic container from other food source, (such as sour cream), washed and cleaned out.

CHAI SMOOTHIE

- 2 T. ND (non-dairy) creamer
- ¾ C. *Light* Coconut Milk (or your choice ND milk substitute)
- 1.5 C frozen chopped Spinach
- 2 T. fresh cilantro (opt.)
- 1 avocado
- ½ C. Chai Concentrate (I like Oregon Chai)
- 1.5 C. frozen Berries (I like Wyman's Triple Berry Blend)

To Make: Put all ingredients into a blender. Add Light Coconut milk or ND milk substitute of your choice. Then, add enough water to just cover all the ingredients and blend until smooth.

PRESTO! WG PESTO PASTA

- WG (Whole Grain) Corkscrew or bowtie pasta
- 4–5 T. Homemade Basil-Cilantro Pasto from above
- As many Cherry tomatoes as you like, halved
- Sprinkle of Pine Nuts to taste (opt.)

To Make: Cook pasta to al dente. Add pesto while hot—stir until thoroughly mixed. Toss in halved cherry tomatoes sprinkle with pine nuts.

WESTERN BEAN & RICE BOWL

- 1 can seasoned black beans (or your beans of choice)
- Red and/or Green Salsa (I like Goya medium Salsa Verde and Pace Picante sauce Medium)
- Red Enchilada Sauce (opt.)
- 10oz. can diced tomatoes and green chilies
- ½ of a 6oz. can large Pitted Black Olives, drained
- Enough Tostitos Scoops Chips—or other plain corn/tortilla chip
- < 2 T. SC (opt.)
- < 2 T. sprinkle of shredded cheese (opt.)
- 1 C. cooked WG Rice

To Make: Cook rice in rice cooker or follow instruction for stovetop and set aside. Pour can of beans and can of diced tomatoes and green chilies into bowl. Sprinkle less than 2 T. cheese on top if desired. Add optional Enchilada sauce as well at this point. Cover with saran wrap and microwave 3 minutes until piping hot. Add cup of cooked WG rice and dollop of less than 2 T. sour cream, if desired. Spoon into Tostito scoop chips and eat that way . . . or crunch up other plain corn or tortilla chips into beans and eat with a spoon.

If Cooking For Family and/or Spouse: Simply double or triple above ingredients to suit number of people cooking for. Add a little cooked ground beef, (just to theirs), if you think it would add appeal.

ASIAN VEGETABLE/RICE BOWL

- 1 C. Brown Rice—cooked
- Chili Garlic Sauce (opt.)
- 16oz. frozen Stir-Fry Vegetables

- 8.25 can Beets
- ½ C. + 2 T. Stir-Fry Sauce (I like KIKKOMAN stir-fry sauce)

To Make: Cook rice in rice cooker or according to stovetop directions. In a saucepan combine frozen stir-fry vegetables, can of beets, and stir-fry sauce. Sauté until veggies are tender—about 10–15 minutes. Add rice to sauté pan of veggies and combine thoroughly. Serve w/ chili garlic sauce on top for some kick, but be careful . . . a little bit goes a long ways!

- 2 T. extra virgin olive oil
- 2–3 Cups Mixed Greens
- 4 tsp. honey
- 1 avocado—peeled, pitted, sliced

- 1 T. apple cider vinegar
- 12 strawberries, sliced
- 1 tsp. lemon juice
- ½ C. chopped pecans (or walnuts)

To Make: Mix together EVOO, honey, apple cider vinegar, and lemon juice in small bowl. Toss the rest of the ingredients in a larger bowl. Drizzle the salad dressing over the Salad. Sprinkle with pecans. Serve with warm bread and less than 1 T. butter if desired.

VERSATILE, ANY NIGHT OF THE WEEK SALAD

- 2–3 C. Mixed Greens (spinach, kale, arugula, red/green lettuce, etc.)
- 2 C. chopped Vegetables (tomatoes, carrots, bell peppers, cucumber, avocado, broccoli, radishes, etc.)
- 2–3 T. seeds or nuts (your choice of pumpkin seed, flax seed, sunflower seed, pine nuts, walnuts, pecans, etc.)
- 2 T. dried cranberries or raisins (opt.)

To Make: Get creative with your bad self! Choose whatever combinations appeal to you of fresh salad greens, vegetables, seeds and/or nuts and toss them all together in a big bowl. Drizzle your favorite store bought Vinaigrette or make one of the homemade recipes included above or below. Remember to stay away from mayonnaise based salad dressings such as ranch, blue cheese, thousand island, as these tend to have too much of the stuff that's not allowed. But most vinaigrettes or Italian salad dressings are perfectly fine and taste better anyways!

PERFECT ASIAN VINAIGRETTE

- 3 T. extra virgin olive oil
- 1 tsp. natural sea salt
- 1 T. white sugar
- 1 tsp. black pepper
- 1 T. brown sugar
- 1 T. soy sauce
- 3 tsp. honey

- ½ T. balsamic vinegar
- ½ T. red wine vinegar
- 1 tsp. sesame oil
- ½ T. balsamic vinegar
- 1 tsp. lemon juice
- 1 T. Dijon mustard

To Make: Combine all ingredients in a bowl. Store in a pickle jar (or other comparable sized jar or plastic container) in the fridge. Drizzle over whatever kind of salad you make for a gourmet, rich meal! This is a strong dressing, so a little goes a long way. Save the rest for future salads! Serve with side of bakery fresh bread smothered with less than 1 tablespoon of butter.

HOLIDAY VINAIGRETTE

- 4 T. extra virgin olive oil
- 1 tsp. natural sea salt
- 1 T. white sugar
- ½ tsp. cayenne pepper
- 1 T. brown sugar
- ½ tsp. paprika
- 3 tsp. honey
- ¼ tsp. cloves
- 1 tsp. cinnamon
- 1 tsp. pumpkin pie spice
- ½ tsp. nutmeg
- ½ T. cocoa—natural unsweetened

To Make: Combine all ingredients in a bowl. Store in a pickle jar (or other comparable sized jar or plastic container) in the fridge. Drizzle over whatever kind of salad you make for a gourmet, rich meal! This is a poignant, highly spiced dressing, so a little goes a long way. Save the rest for future salads! Serve with side of bakery fresh bread smothered with less than 1 tablespoon of butter.

PORTABELLA N' PESTO MUSHROOM BURGER

Makes 2 Servings

- 2 Hamburger Buns
- 1 big tomato sliced into rings
- 8 oz. pkg. whole Portabella Mushrooms
- 3 T. Extra virgin
- Homemade Basil-Cilantro Pesto (from before)
- Olive oil
- Seasoned salt & pepper

To Make: Drizzle half of olive oil into sauté pan. Cut each whole portabella mushroom down the middle—it's okay if it falls apart a little! Sauté 10–15 minutes flipping regularly, and adding more olive oil as needed until limp, squishy and very appetizing looking. Sprinkle generously with seasoned salt and pepper. Meanwhile, while mushrooms are cooking, spread pesto generously on both sides of both buns. Put one tomato slice on each bun. Place cooked portabella on top of tomato slices. Serve w/ pickle on the side.

If Making for Family or Spouse: Leave out pesto and replace with condiments of mustard, ketchup, or mayonnaise. Add cooked hamburger patties to just theirs. O, and buy one additional 8 oz. package portabellas!

HOMEMADE SMOOTHIE

- 1.5 C. frozen Berry Blend
- 1 T. Natural Unsweetened Cocoa
- 1/3 C. Silk or Soft Tofu (opt.)
- 2 tsp. vanilla extract
- 1.5 C. frozen chopped Spinach
- 1.5 T. Peanut butter
- 1 avocado or 1 banana, interchangeable
- ½ T. Honey
- 1.5 C. Lite Coconut milk (or your choice ND milk)

To Make: Put all ingredients in a blender. Add Coconut milk (or ND substitute of your choice such as Soy, Almond, Rice, or Oat milk). Fill the rest of the blender up with water, until the water just covers the ingredients. Blend until smooth.

SWEET POTATO CURRY PLUS

- 1 C. Organic *Lite* Coconut Milk
- 3 big carrots
- 15 oz. jar Curry Simmer Sauce [I used Patak's Original Dopiaza Curry]
- 1 orange bell pepper
- 1 tomato
- 2 Sweet Potatoes

To Make: **Preheat oven to 450.** Bake sweet potatoes on foil at 450 degrees for 65 minutes, or until done; when a fork slides easily in and out. Just before sweet potatoes are done baking pour coconut milk in Saucepan. Take sweet potatoes out of oven, peel off skin, and mash and stir into coconut milk that is now heated. Adjust to low/medium heat. Cut the sweet potatoes into smaller pieces using a fork and then mash w/ potato masher. Add chopped carrots, bell pepper, and tomato. Let simmer 15 more minutes, or until hot. *If Cooking for Family or Spouse:* While potatoes are cooking, brown 1 pound ground beef in frying pan and set aside. Simply add this to just theirs.

IRANIAN STREET TACOS

- Mini Golden Blend Street Tacos [I like Don Pancho's mini corn tortillas]
- Hummus
- Sun-dried tomatoes
- 2 Jalapeno Olives (or whatever kind of olive you like)

To Make: Take 1 mini corn tortilla and smear it on one side with hummus. Put on some sundried tomatoes and a few jalapeno-stuffed olives, or whatever kind olive you like. Fold in half into a little street taco and eat. Make as many as you need.

CAJUN GUMBO

- 15oz. can seasoned Black Beans
- 1.5 T maple Syrup
- 15oz. can Pinto beans
- 1 C. cooked WG Rice
- 1.5 tsp. minced garlic (or 1 large clove crushed in press)
- 1 C. Pasta or Tomato sauce
- ½–1 T. Cajun seasoning (depending on how spicy you want it)
- 1/3 C. Hot Banana pepper rings
- 1–1.5lb. Salmon fillet [if cooking for family/spouse]
- Squirt of lemon juice

To Make: Put everything (besides salmon fillet if you are cooking for someone else as well) in pan over medium heat. Heat up and mix together until bubbling. Add less than 2 T. shredded cheese if desirable. Transfer to bowls. Serve with less than 2 T. sour cream on top, salsa, and WG chips, if desirable. *If Cooking for Family or Spouse:* Sprinkle Salmon with Extra Virgin olive oil and salt and pepper. Preheat Oven to 500 degrees broil. Bake for approximately 8–10 minutes or until tender. Serve on top the other people's bowls of Gumbo, enjoying your own!

CHICKPEA PESTO DELIGHT

- 15.5oz. can Chick peas/Garbanzo beans
- 4–5 T. Homemade Basil-Cilantro Pesto (from before)
- < 2 T. parmesan shredded cheese
- 1/8 tsp. ground white pepper
- ¼ tsp. crushed red pepper

To Make: Pour can of Chickpeas into bowl. Sprinkle with parmesan and spices. Heat in microwave 3 minutes. Mix well. Add homemade Pesto from before and mix really well while still piping hot. Enjoy!

WG PASTA ITALIAN VEGETABLE BOWL

- ½ T. Oregano
- ¼ tsp. ground/rubbed Sage
- ½ tsp. basil leaves
- ¼ tsp. Thyme
- 24oz. Pasta Sauce
- Whole Wheat Rotini noodles
- 16oz. Frozen Vegetable medley

To Make: Boil large pot of water for noodles. When it's boiling add noodles and frozen veggies. Cook until al dente—about 10 to 15 minutesor until noodles are tender (it's okay if veggies are not completely tender). Drain water. While pasta is cooking, put pasta sauce in a saucepan. Adjust heat to low. Add all the spices to sauce. Stir thoroughly. Add the cooked rice to the noodles and vegetables; pour sauce over and Voila. . . bon appetite!

TRI-BEANS & RICE

- 15oz. can Black Beans
- 8oz. can Water Chestnuts
- 15oz. can European soldier beans
- tsp. Chipotle Chili spice
- 15oz. can Pinquito beans
- 8oz. can tomato sauce
- ½ C. cooked brown rice
- 1.5 T. lemon juice
- ½ C. Wild Rice mix
- 1.5 tsp. minced garlic (or 1 large clove pressed)
- 1 C. water
- 15oz. can corn
- 1 ¾ T. Cajun seasoning

To Make: Cook Rice in rice cooker or according to stovetop directions on package. Set aside. Combine all the rest of the ingredients in a big bowl. Add rice and combine. Microwave for 4–5 minutes. Serve hot. Garnish with less than 2 T. shredded cheese, SC, salsa and WG chips if you like.

WG PASTA SALAD

- 1 lb. (16oz.) WG Penne, Rotini (corkscrew), Bowtie, Fusilli Pasta
- 1/3 C. thinly sliced green onion
- 1 C. sliced bell pepper (1 medium)
- 1 C. zucchini thin (1/2 medium)
- 1/3 C. sliced banana peppers (opt.)
- 1 C. halved cherry tomatoes
- 1 C. olives chopped

Dressing:

- 1/3 C. red wine vinegar
- ½ C. Extra virgin olive oil
- ½ tsp. natural sea salt
- ½ T. Dijon mustard
- ¾ tsp. pepper
- 1 small clove garlic pressed, or ½ tsp. minced
- 1 tsp. oregano
- ½ C. Extra virgin olive oil
- little squirt lemon juice
- 5 T. juice from banana pepper jar (opt.)
- 4 T. Capers (opt.)

To Make: Combine all the ingredients for the Dressing in a big plastic bowl. Add the chopped vegetables to the dressing and thoroughly coat. Cook noodles in big pot of boiling water until al dente. Drain pasta and add to dressed vegetables in the bowl. Combine everything thoroughly and wait hours until you can eat it! Also, pasta salad is phenomenal when refrigerated a few days so don't hesitate to make a bunch and have for a meal in a week.

ZATARAIN'S JUMBALAYA

- 1 Box Zatarain's Jumbalaya
- 1 can red kidney beans
- 1 pkg. Sausage (if cooking for kids/spouse)

To Make: Mix 3 ¾ cups water, RICE MIX, 2 T. olive or vegetable oil in 3-quart saucepan. Bring to boil. Reduce heat to low and add can of beans. Cover and simmer 25 minutes or until rice is tender. Serve w/ WG chips salsa, and a dollop of less than 2 T. sour cream if desirable.

If Cooking for Family or Spouse: While Jumbalaya is cooking, bring water to boil in other pot. Add as much sausage as you think your people need. Cook for 10 minutes on medium/high, or until done when cut open. Cut sausage up and add just to their bowls.

GREEK STREET TACOS

- Mini street tacos—Golden Corn Tortilla [I like Don Poncho]
- Hummus
- 1 cucumber, diced and chopped into long, narrow pieces
- Cherry tomatoes, halved
- Olives, as many as you like [I prefer kalamata]
- Small bunch chives—chopped green onion

To make: Spread hummus over little, mini golden corn street tortillas. Sprinkle chopped green onion chives directly onto hummus, so it sticks. Peel cucumber, cut in half, and slice into long, thin pieces. Lay 3-4 long, narrow sticks of cucumber in middle of tortilla. Add as many halved cherry tomatoes as looks good. Finish with some of your favorite dark olives. Fold in half to make taco and enjoy!

GREAT LENT FAST FORTY-DAY SAMPLE MEAL PLAN

PB=Peanut Butter, WG=Whole Grain, SC=Sour Cream, ND=Non-Dairy, *Amy's* Soups= Favorite brand of Healthy Canned soup

Day	Breakfast	Lunch	Dinner	Snack
1	X	X	- Bowl of *Amy's* Golden Lentils Soup w/ 1 Tbsp. SC - 2 pieces bread w/ 1 Tbsp. butter - Strawberries	20oz. Green Juice or V8
2	X	X	- WG Pasta w/ Basil-Cilantro Pesto *** - 1 Piece of bread w/ 1 Tbsp. butter - Sliced Apple w/ PB	20oz. Green Juice or V8
3	X	X	- Homemade Chai Smoothie *** - Bowl of Granola w/ Non-Dairy milk & Blueberries - Some Mixed Nuts	20oz. Green Juice or V8
4	X	X	- Western Beans & Rice Bowl *** - W/ 2 Tbsp. SC & Salsa - Tortilla Chips	20oz. Green Juice or V8
5	X	X	- Asian Vegetable/Rice Bowl ***	20oz. Green Juice or V8
6	X	X	- Bowl of Soup - 2 pieces bakery bread w/ 1 T. butter - Banana w/ PB	20oz. Green Juice or V8
7	X	X	- Homemade Salad w/ dressing *** - 2 Pieces bakery bread w/ 1 T. butter on each - Some Nuts on side	20oz. Green Juice or V8
8	X	X	- Western Beans & Rice Bowl w/ 2 Tbsp. SC & Salsa - Tortilla Chips	20oz. Green Juice or V8

9	X	X	- Homemade Salad w/ dressing - 2 Pieces bakery bread w/ 1 T. butter on each - Some Nuts on side	20oz. Green Juice or V8
10	X	X	- Portabella Mushroom Sandwich *** - 1 Dill Pickle -Baby carrots & 2 T. Blue Cheese dressing for dip	20oz. Green Juice or V8
11	X	X	- Homemade Smoothie *** - Big Bowl of Grape Nuts w/ Non-Dairy milk & Blueberries - Some Mixed Nuts	20oz. Green Juice or V8
12	X	X	- Iranian Street Tacos *** - ½ Apple w/ PB	20oz. Green Juice or V8
13	X	X	- Bowl of *Amy's* Split Pea Soup w/ 1 Tbsp. SC - 2 pieces bread w/ 1 Tbsp. butter - Strawberries	20oz. Green Juice or V8
14	X	X	- Cajun Gumbo *** - Side of plain WG Tortilla rolled up	20oz. Green Juice or V8
15	X	X	- Homemade Salad w/ dressing *** - 2 Pieces bakery bread w/ 1 T. butter on each - Some Nuts on side	20oz. Green Juice or V8
16	X	X	- Sweet Potato Curry Plus *** - 1 Piece bakery bread w/ 1 T. butter	20oz. Green Juice or V8
17	X	X	- Western Beans & Rice Bowl*** w/ 2 Tbsp. SC & Salsa - Tortilla Chips	20oz. Green Juice or V8
18	X	X	- Asian Vegetable/Rice Bowl***	20oz. Green Juice or V8

19	X	X	- Bowl of *Amy's* Minestrone Soup w/ 1 Tbsp. SC - 2 pieces bread w/ 1 Tbsp. butter - Strawberries	20oz. Green Juice or V8
20	X	X	- WG Italian Pasta/Vegetable Bowl - 1 Piece bakery bread w/ 1 T. butter	20oz. Green Juice or V8
21	X	X	- Homemade Smoothie - Big Bowl of Grape Nuts w/ ND milk & Blueberries - Some mixed Nuts	20oz. Green Juice or V8
22	X	X	- Pasta Salad *** - 1 piece bakery bread w/ 1 T. butter	20oz. Green Juice or V8
23	X	X	- Bowl of *Amy's* Lentil Soup w/ 1 Tbsp. SC - 2 pieces bread w/ 1 Tbsp. butter (opt.) - Strawberries	20oz. Green Juice or V8
24	X	X	- Homemade Salad w/ dressing - 2 Pieces bakery bread w/ 1 T. butter on each - Some Nuts on side	20oz. Green Juice or V8
25	X	X	- Asian Vegetable/Rice Bowl	20oz. Green Juice or V8
26	X	X	- Homemade Smoothie - Bowl Oatmeal w/ Tbsp. brown sugar & Raisins - Some mixed Nuts	20oz. Green Juice or V8
27	X	X	- Chickpea Pesto Delight *** - 1 Roma tomato sliced up w/ pepper on Side	20oz. Green Juice or V8
28	X	X	- Tri-Beans & Rice *** w/ 2 Tbsp. SC & Salsa - WG Chips	20oz. Green Juice or V8

29	X	X	- Zatarain's Jumbalaya *** w/ 2 T. SC (opt.) & Salsa - WG Chips	20oz. Green Juice or V8
30	X	X	- Homemade Smoothie - Bowl Favorite WG Cereal w/ ND Milk & Blueberries - Some mixed Nuts	20oz. Green Juice or V8
31	X	X	- WG Italian Pasta/Vegetable Bowl - 1 Piece bakery bread w/ 1 T. butter	20oz. Green Juice or V8
32	X	X	- Bowl of *Your Favorite* Soup w/ 1 Tbsp. SC (opt.) - 2 pieces bread w/ 1 Tbsp. butter - Strawberries	20oz. Green Juice or V8
33	X	X	- Western Beans & Rice Bowl w/ 2 T. SC & Salsa - Tortilla Chips	20oz. Green Juice or V8
34	X	X	- Homemade Salad w/ dressing - 2 Pieces bakery bread w/ 1 T. butter on each - Some Nuts on side	20oz. Green Juice or V8
35	X	X	- Asian Vegetable/Rice Bowl	20oz. Green Juice or V8
36	X	X	- Bowl of *Your Favorite* Soup w/ 1 Tbsp. SC - 2 pieces bread w/ 1 Tbsp. butter - Strawberries	20oz. Green Juice or V8
37	X	X	- Homemade Salad w/ dressing - 2 Pieces bakery bread w/ 1 T. butter on each - Some Nuts on side	20oz. Green Juice or V8
38	X	X	- Western Beans & Rice Bowl w/ 2 Tbsp. SC & Salsa - Tortilla Chips	20oz. Green Juice or V8

| 39 | X | X | - Homemade Smoothie
- Bowl Favorite WG Cereal w/ ND Milk & Blueberries
- Some mixed Nuts | 20oz. Green Juice or V8 |
| 40 | X | X | - Greek Street Tacos ***
- ½ Apple w/ PB | 20oz. Green Juice or V8 |

Remember, this is just a *sample* meal plan. View each of these days as auspicious cards that you can play with and rearrange in any order you want. Use some, reuse them, discard others, rearrange them ... repeat meals galore. Whatever works best for you!

BIBLIOGRAPHY

Akrotirianakis. "And When You Fast." http://www.goarch.org/-/and-when-you-fast-?inherityRedirect=true.
Anonymous. *Twenty-Four Hours A Day*. Mansfield Centre, CT: Martino, 2011.
Cowman, L.B. *Streams in the Desert*. Grand Rapids, MI: Zondervan, 1996.
Demos, Father Athanasios. "Focus Fasting: A Reflection on the Great Fast." http://www.goarch.org/-/focus-fasting-a-reflection-on-the-great-fast?inherityRedirect=true.
"The Fasting Rule of the Orthodox Church—Exceptions." http://www.abbamoses.com/fasting.html.
Gregory, Susan. *The Daniel Fast*. Carol Stream, Illinois: Tyndale Momentum, 2010.
The Holy Bible, English Standard Version, ESV. Wheaton, Illinois: Crossway, 2001.
The Holy Bible, New International Version, NIV. Colorado Springs, Colorado: Biblica Inc., 1984.
Maximos, Metropolitan. "On Fasting." http://www.goarch.org/-/on-fasting?inheritRedirect=true.
Papageorgiou, Rev. Fr. Panayiotis. "Fasting: Is It Really Necessary?" http://www.goarch.org/-/fasting-is-it-really-necessary-?inherityRedirect=true.
Piper, John. *A Hunger for God: Desiring God through Fasting and Prayer*. Wheaton, Illinois: Crossway, 1997.
St Symeon. "Sayings on Fasting—St Symeon the New Theologian." http://www.abbamoses.com/fasting.html.
Wallis, Arthur. *God's Chosen Fast*. Fort Washington, PA: Christian Literature Crusade, 1968.

www.ingramcontent.com/pod-product-compliance
Lightning Source LLC
Chambersburg PA
CBHW060559230426
43670CB00011B/1895